Don
CRIST

Running Wild

RUNNING

Through the Grand Canyon

Harbinger House

TUCSON

WILD

on the Ancient Path

JOHN ANNERINO

Foreword by Charles Bowden

Photographs by Christine Keith

The events and characters in this book are real, but the names of several people have been changed to protect their privacy.

HARBINGER HOUSE, INC.
Tucson, Arizona

© 1992 John Annerino
Photographs © 1992 Christine Keith
Foreword © 1992 Charles Bowden
All rights reserved

Manufactured in the United States of America
∞ This book was printed on acid-free, archival-quality paper
Typeset in 11 point Linotron 202 Sabon
Designed by Harrison Shaffer

10   9   8   7   6   5   4   3   2   1

Library of Congress Cataloging-in-Publication Data
Annerino, John.
    Running wild : through the Grand Canyon on the ancient path /
John Annerino ; photographs by Christine Keith ; foreword by Charles
Bowden.
        p.   cm.
    Includes bibliographical references.
    ISBN 0-943173-83-3 (alk.) : $11.95
        1. Running—Arizona—Grand Canyon. 2. Grand Canyon (Ariz.)—
Description and travel. 3. Indian trails—Arizona. I. Title.
GV1061.22.A6A56   1992
796.42 ' 09791 ' 32—dc20   92-25214

For Tim and Craig

Without them, this journey
would not have been possible.

Contents

Off the Rim and into the Heart of Stone

He is running down a trail in the mountains, and there is no one there. He is running across a desert flat in the heat of midday, and there is no one there. Once it is the Sierra Estrellas, a hard-rock spine under burning desert sun near Phoenix. He leaps from rock to rock, the water is never enough, his body hurts, and still he runs on. Or it is the Grand Canyon, the Chiricahuas, the San Francisco Peaks, always running. A man of average stature, the smile flashing easily, the body trained to do what it is told, and inside his head these strange ideas of adventures, adventures to be made by foot, a world that demands running.

John Annerino was raised in Phoenix and fled to Prescott to recover from this gruesome fact. I first met him when he began popping into the office where I worked for a small magazine, and he had these ideas about places he should run. He would cross the terrain, take photographs of what he saw, and then write a story. The magazine, he explained, would pay him. He talked with great animation of these plans, his voice rising and falling. The idea would be laid out not so much as a query about a possible story but more like he was offering me a chance to buy into a racehorse. Of course, I was to print the story. And why not, he'd note, since his photography was already being published in Japan, Italy, Germany, France, and the United States—lurking out there somewhere beyond the hallowed Southwest. Who could resist, since this horse always won and never failed to go the distance. He was the running man.

There is a kind of madness that infects certain lucky souls in the Southwest, a lunacy wherein the point of life is less to plot a career than to get into the country, to hustle and cajole the wherewithal for that next trek, probe, adventure. A lot of boats hit the white water, boots march down the trail, and running shoes race across the sierras, borne along by this madness. People disguise this condition by claiming they are photographers, writers, scientists, all manner of allegedly honorable callings. Do not be fooled. There is a simple test to expose them for what they are: they will not leave the place; they refuse to advance up career ladders that threaten them with plush jobs in distant cities. Money cannot sway them—unless their boots have worn out. Instead they plot, like highwaymen in the dark of night, elaborate scenarios that will enable them to remain here and do what they want to do. Which is always the same: go into the country, deeper and deeper. The late Edward Abbey was a model of this type, but they are everywhere, skulking about and wearing various disguises. In order to live this life, one must have soul, a penchant for larceny, and an absolute lust for this dry ground that others look at with fear and apprehension. I must be ruthless on this point because I am absolutely certain about this type—I have to look at one of the beasts every morning when I shave.

Once Annerino came into my office and, as I suspected he would, sprang his latest project on me. He had a simple idea: he was going to run on trails across Arizona, south to north from Mexico to Utah. Like all such rascals, he had hung this sting on some kind of pretext. I believe he wanted to see and photograph this wild ground the way the Indians and pioneers once saw it. But that was all a smoke screen. I knew what he wanted, what we all want. What really glinted in his eyes was the idea of floating down trails day after day, crossing mountains, dropping in and out of canyons, eating up all the country alone. Naturally, I bought into this madness, he did the run, and it all splashed across the page with words and pictures.

Like all such people in this part of the country, Annerino keeps returning to the Grand Canyon. If you wonder why, then you must never have been there. And if you have not been there, put down this book and go right now. No doubt you've read somewhere about how long it is and how deep it is and how old the rocks are. I am sure these are important matters. But what really counts is that the Canyon is a huge hole and when one goes into it, the world falls away. The ears start listening to the rocks, and thoughts flood out that before were not permitted. When this happens often enough, after years and years of dropping off the rim and going into the heart of stone, well, then the change begins to happen, one that no one is ever quite prepared for.

Running, running across the rock plateaus, the trail undulating, the body warmed up, the mind . . . well, the mind seems to be doing nothing but existing. The huge walls of the Canyon encircle; there is silence everywhere except for the pounding of the feet, but even this sound seems to vanish and the body glides as if by magic across the ground. Pain? It is always a possibility, but it seems hardly to matter. Destinations also fade away because the very goal of the run turns out to be this exact instant. At these moments the only time that exists is flashing on that digital watch on the wrist, and this time, though accurate, has ceased to tell one anything. Now the dead begin to appear, the Indians whose language no one knows, the Spaniards wearing those awkward leather vests, the early prospectors, the strange beasts that vanished ten thousand or twenty thousand years ago. Scientists tell us that such experiences occur because the mind under the stress of running is being bathed in a kind of natural morphine produced by the body. Could be, but who cares? No one who has had these experiences ever desires a tidy explanation anymore than one craves a scientific dissection of the emotion we all call love.

This is a book about such experiences in such places. It is about going into the country the only way that seems to work—on foot. For Annerino, it is an effort to discover what exactly happened to him out there. For us, it is a fantasy. Our legs are light, our feet are flying, and we glide, truly glide, over the roll of the land. The sun is up, the air is fresh, the stone is old, and we are free and at peace and the clocks have stopped because another kind of time has taken over, one where the dead can speak and nothing ever really dies. The Canyon, well, they tell us the Canyon is called Grand, but we have moved past such words. Our feet are taking us right into the stone.

CHARLES BOWDEN

Running Wild

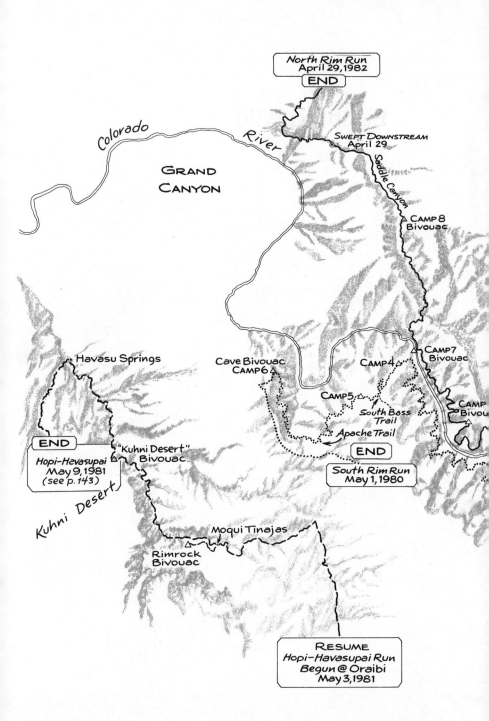

Drawn by Michael Taylor

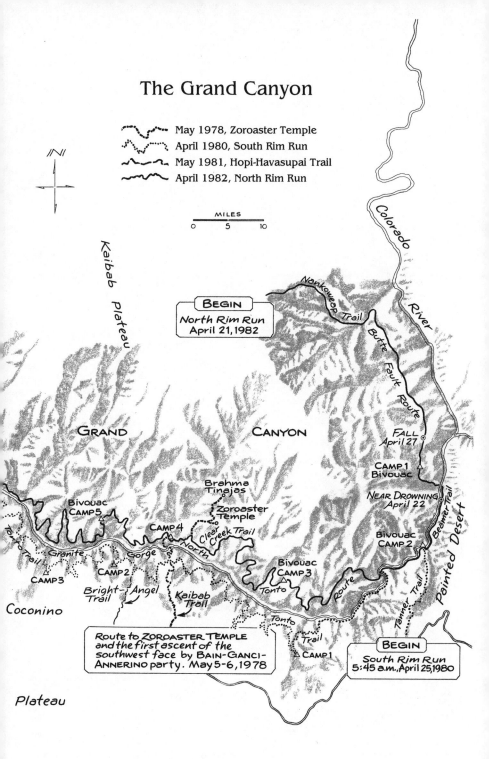

The Grand Canyon

May 1978, Zoroaster Temple
April 1980, South Rim Run
May 1981, Hopi-Havasupai Trail
April 1982, North Rim Run

MILES

0   5   10

N

Kaibab Plateau

Colorado River

Nankoweep Trail

BEGIN
North Rim Run
April 21, 1982

Butte Fault Route

GRAND   CANYON

FALL
April 27

CAMP 1
Bivouac

NEAR DROWNING
April 22

Brahma
Tinajas

Zoroaster
Temple

BIVOUAC
CAMP 2

Beamer Trail

Bivouac
CAMP 5

Painted Desert

CAMP 4

Clear Creek Trail

Granite   *Gorge*   *North*

Tonto

Bivouac
CAMP 3

Tenner Trail

Tonto Trail

CAMP 2

Route

**Tonto*

Bright-Angel Trail

Kaibab Trail

CAMP 3

Coconino

Tonto Trail

CAMP 1

Route to **ZOROASTER TEMPLE**
and the first ascent of the
southwest face by **BAIN-GANCI-**
ANNERINO party. May 5-6, 1978

BEGIN
South Rim Run
5:45 a.m., April 25, 1980

Plateau

*Natural Selection has designed us . . .
for a career of seasonal journeys
on foot through a blistering land
of thornscrub . . . desert.*

Bruce Chatwin, *The Songlines*

CHAPTER ONE

"You'll Never Run Again"

The closer you get to death,
The clearer the image of life.

the late Roger Marshall
Himalayan climber

I am falling, uncontrollably. I'm not sure how far, but
when I hit I know I'm going to die. At any moment I'll
bounce on the end of my rope, the fragile anchors will rip
out of the rotten crack, and I'll slam brutally against the
jagged rocks below—my helmet crushed, my back broken,
my lungs punctured with splintered bones and choked with
blood. It'd happened to better climbers than myself, and
now it is happening to me. And there is nothing I can do
about it except scream as I plunge backward, still clutching
the broken handhold in my left hand.

The day hadn't started out that way. It was a spring-
warm winter morning in the Valley of the Sun when Tony
Mangine and I decided to postpone a long-awaited climbing
trip to Granite Mountain a hundred miles north. Camelback
Mountain was only minutes away in the heart of metro-
politan Phoenix, and we hoped it would offer us a challenging new climbing route as well as a much needed break
from teaching and traveling. As an outdoor instructor at a

local community college, I'd been in the boonies virtually every weekend of the previous seven months teaching climbing and wilderness survival, and I was starting to burn out. So I looked forward to a day of climbing alone with a friend.

It was a leisurely Saturday morning. The balmy desert air was still heavy with the musty scent of orange blossoms. Coveys of quail ran frantically back and forth across the trail in front of us as Tony and I trudged up the steep climber's route through Echo Canyon. We had made the same trip many times before, leading students up a spectacular finger of rock called The Monk. But today we'd eyed a stiff crack climb ominously called Suicide Direct. We'd heard it wasn't a particularly difficult route overall, but the crux move out of a small overhang was committing and needed to be protected by placing "bombproof anchors" just below the crux.

I felt confident as we both roped up, and didn't pay much attention to three members of a local rescue team practicing rope maneuvers on another route nearby.

"On belay?" I said to Tony as I buckled on my helmet.

"On belay," he said, carefully holding the nylon rope tied to me.

"Climb?" I said, double-checking his belay.

"Climb!" he said.

I scrambled up a short apron of dark conglomerate rock that ended atop an awkward ledge at the base of the small alcove, or overhang. I put in a nut, clipped a carabiner to it, and fed the rope through it. "I'm in," I yelled down to Tony; in the parlance of rock climbers, it was a way to let your belayer know that you had your first anchor in, so that if you fell he'd be able to catch you before you hit the ground.

I looked up. The crack arched above me out of the overhang to the crux move thirty feet above. Before continuing, I looked for a solid place to put the next anchor in, somewhere midway between the crux and the prow of rock I was standing on.

"Watch me, Tone," I yelled down, "I want to get some bomber protection in before doing it."

"I gotcha!"

I climbed up a few feet and slotted a small nut alongside a chockstone wedged into a V-shaped crack. Tenuously perched, I tugged at the aluminum nut to see whether it was secure; from its placement, I realized that if I fell off the crux the force of the fall could pull it out—and I'd take a grounder. Quickly, I slotted in another nut on the opposite side of the chockstone to counterbalance the first nut. I tugged at it to set it in place. Once I did, I was confident the two nuts would hold a short fall—if the chockstone didn't pull out. I carefully down-climbed back to the alcove and then rehearsed in my head the sequence of moves I'd need to make in order to reach the safety of the anchor bolt just above the crux.

"Ready, Tone?" I yelled. I took a deep breath.

"I gotcha."

I started up again, promising myself not to go for the crux above my anchors unless I could safely reverse the moves in the event I didn't make it on the first try. A few quick moves brought me back to my high point, and I realized my palms were sweaty. I continued up, my feet jammed in the crack below, my left arm stretched out as far as I could reach, my right hand groping for another hold. Just inch up a little more, I told myself. Suddenly I was struck by just how rotten the rock felt as it crumbled beneath my feet. Doing a difficult move on glacier-polished Yosemite granite was one thing, but doing a hard move on grungy desert rock was another. You couldn't always rely on it.

A sickening feeling came over me when I realized just how exposed I'd be if I continued the last few feet to the crux. I'd nervously climbed too high too quickly to safely reverse my moves, and I no longer trusted my life to the two shaky anchors below. My only hope was to smoothly negotiate the crux and clip into the bolt above. If the rest of the climb looked this rotten I'd rappel off and call it a day, head for Granite Mountain and some real rock.

As I stretched for the crux, my right leg started trembling; I had "sewing machine" leg. I was gripped with fear, and I couldn't stop my leg from shaking. I was about to peel off when I made a desperate reach for the hold with my left hand. I fingered it, and felt the course grains of sand behind it. I had it, and I breathed a sigh of relief as I pulled down on it with all my strength in order to mantle on top of it. As I did, it broke off.

And suddenly I am falling backward, still clutching the rotten hold in my hand. I scream with terror because I'm going to die. But before I do I have to warn Tony to brace himself for the tremendous impact of the fall: "AGGHHHHHHH!!!"

The grisly details of exactly how I am going to die, not the image of my family, flashes before me as I hit a small protrusion of rock with the impact of a body being thrown off the roof of a three-story building. I scream again when I hit, long mournful wails, then spin around, hanging there in midair at the end of the rope. One nut slides down the rope and smacks me in the face; it has ripped out. So I know that at any moment the other nut will pull out and I'll plummet the rest of the way to the ground.

I look down to see how much farther I have to fall before I die, but I am more horrified to see the grotesque shape of my left ankle. The sole of my climbing boot is facing me; worse, the tibia is about to tear through the wafer-white skin. I start whimpering, waiting for the life-saving nut to rip—and to end the excruciating pain. Instead,

I continue swaying at the end of the rope, overcome with nausea and pain.

"John, are you all right?" Tony knows I'm not; even from his stance I know he can see my mangled left foot.

"Tone, you got me?" I shriek. My breathing is shallow and frantic.

"I got you. What do you want me to do?"

Tony is holding all my weight with his bare hands, and I know he won't drop me if he can help it. But I'm terrified that if the tiny metal nut miraculously holds while he lowers me, the slightest jarring will cause my ankle bone to puncture my leg like a stone knife from the inside out, and I'll bleed to death long before I reach the ground.

"Tone! You've got to lower me! . . . carefully! . . . or the nut will rip!"

"Tell me when you're ready!"

"Okay, easy!" On the verge of panic, whimpering from pain, I tuck my left leg behind me in hopes of protecting it during the descent. I splay my two hands above me, my right hip against the wall; by using the friction of my body against the rock wall, I hope to relieve some of the tension on the nut.

"Easy, Tone! I don't think I'm going to make it!" Tears are running down my cheeks and snot is dribbling out of my nose.

"You'll make it!"

I know the weight on the rope is oppressive for Tony to hold, but if anybody can lower me through the overhang without dropping me like a stone it is Tony.

The abrasive rock tears the palms of my hands and scrapes viciously at my bruised right hip, but the ground slowly, painfully gets closer and closer until Tony sets me down as if he's lowering me onto eggshells.

Still sniveling and moaning from the agonizing pain, I

look up at my friend and at the rescue team now gathered around me. I can tell by their startled expressions I'm in dire straits; it looks to them as if my leg bone will tear through at any moment and a deadly torrent of blood will come gushing out in huge spurts until there is nothing left for my heart to pump. Without thinking about it, I crawl over on my back and start telling people what to do. If I am going to die, it is not going to be without a fight.

"You"—I point to one young climber—"call an ambulance. Tell them we need a litter and men to carry it." I collapse in agony, crying as I bite down on a piece of nylon sling to try to alleviate the pain. "Tone, make sure someone calls my mom—and Anna."

The wait is interminable. The pain is beyond anything I've ever experienced before, a torturous throbbing as if my ankle is being pulverized with a sledgehammer. Tony stands by my side, reassuring me over and over: "You're going to make it, John."

I want to believe him; Tony never lies.

II

The crunch of footsteps and the muffled clang of climbing gear precedes the men who struggle through the underbrush to reach me. "He's over here," I hear someone yell, and soon the men circle around me, blowing like horses from the steep climb. I knew that if somehow my leg bone hadn't blown out the side when Tony lowered me, it'd never make the rugged carry back down to the ambulance, which now seems so impossibly far away.

I drift in and out of consciousness from the pain but rear up and watch, mortified, when the EMT cuts into my boot. I don't want to scream in front of these strangers, so I bite down on the sling again until it feels like my teeth are going to break, but as soon as the medic tries to slide the black boot off my tortured left foot I wail again! Every time he touches my foot I take the fall all over again. And when he wraps the air splint around my leg and blows it up like a blood pressure cuff, it feels like my foot is going to explode. I howl the pain of a dying man and black out.

When I come to, a voice overhead is quietly repeating, "You've got to breathe evenly or you'll go into shock . . . you've got to breathe evenly or you'll go into shock." Obediently, I try to take deep, even breaths, but when I realize I'm being carried down off the mountain, man-handled over rocks, cactus, and brush, I grip the metal rail-ings of the litter in mortal fear that someone will slip; I'll be dropped and a dagger of white bone will rip through my splinted leg.

I black out again and come to when I hear the ear-piercing siren of the ambulance screaming as we careen through traffic. The medic keeps repeating his question un-til it finally registers. "What hospital do you want to go to? What hospital do you want to go to? What hospital do you want to go to?"

"County . . . I don't have insurance."

I try to make peace with the pain by closing my eyes, but the rerun is already playing: my first visit to an emer-gency room years earlier. I'd cracked heads with another kid playing "freeze tag" in our grade school's asphalt play-ground. Fortunately, school was already out so my mom was there to grab me. When she did, she ran into the middle of a Chicago intersection and held up rush-hour traffic until a truck driver saw the blood streaming down my forehead. "Get in, lady," he said, swinging open the door. My mom pushed me over her head and he dragged us both into the cab, before thundering to the hospital in an eighteen-wheel tractor-trailer rig, just like the one my dad drove. But that was only my first trip through the E.R.'s revolving doors, a ritual I often repeated throughout my teens: the time my cousin Johnny tried out his new knife—on me; the back flip off the diving board gone awry; the Friday night cruisers beating me with wrenches. Each time I'd bled like a pig, but each time I was pronounced fit enough to wait the two to three hours it took the trauma specialist to get to me before he sewed me up.

But when I'm rolled through the swinging metal doors of Maricopa County Hospital's emergency room, I know this time is far more serious. The attending physician takes one look at my foot flopped out at the end of the air splint as if it's going to fall off and says, "We've got to reduce this—now."

I'm rushed into an adjoining room, where the doctor, an orthopedic specialist, immediately begins poking my foot with an index finger that feels like a blunt metal spear.

"Does this hurt?"

"Agghhh!"

"How about this?"

"Agghhh!"

"And this?"

"AGGHHH!!"

He leaves the room and returns with two assistants; I have no idea why they are needed until he instructs them to hold me down. They each grab one of my arms. Then I look up at the doctor; he is the size of an NFL fullback and he is about to do the unthinkable. He grabs my foot in his vice-like hands and pulls back on it.

"AGGGGGGGHHHHHHHHHHHHHHH!!!"

He tries again, this time leaning all the way back on his three hundred-pound frame. But his assistants are no match for this brutal round of tug-of-war, and I slide halfway across the table, screaming.

"It's not going back in," he tells his assistants. I am crying and groaning.

"Please," I beg him, "please give me something for the pain." But the doctor and his assistants leave the room without saying a word.

I lie there moaning, "Oh God, help me, please." A sterile dome of light beams down on me and I wonder how much longer the pain will continue. But the nightmare is only beginning. Minutes later, four people file into the room ahead of the doctor. It looks like he's enlisted the help of the maintenance department, because two of the men are dressed in brown. They grip my arms, a third assistant pins my shoulder down, and the fourth holds my leg at the hip.

"Please," I beg him again, "Please give me something for the pain. Please."

"Just relax," he says, and commences another brutal round of tug-of-war.

"AGGGGGGHHHHHHHHHHHHHHH!!!"

"I can't believe it's not going back in," he says, shaking his head. "Prep him for surgery."

I had no idea at the time, but the doctor headed back into the waiting room to get permission from my mother to cut off my foot.

Writhing in pain and drenched in a nervous, foul-smelling sweat, I'm wheeled into an elevator and rushed to another room upstairs, where two nurses begin cutting off my pants. I plead with them, "Please give me something for pain. Please."

"Soon," one of the nurses says; her soft black hand brushes the matted hair off my damp forehead. "Soon."

I'm relieved when it happens so quickly. The anesthesiologist gives me an injection, a gas mask is put over my face, and I am told to count backward.

"Ten, nine, eigh . . . "

When I come to I'm groggy. The pain has not diminished, and my left leg is encased in a sewer-pipe length of plaster from hip to foot. My mom is at my side, whispering, "I wouldn't let them take it off, Son." My mother, thank God! She'd nursed her diabetic mother's gangrenous right foot and had watched doctors amputate first the foot, then the rest of the leg, bit by bit, all the way to the hip; and when gangrene set in in the other foot, their stainless steel saws took away Grandma's life piece by piece. "Sonny-la," Grandma used to call me in her thick German accent, "you go hunting with Grandpa and the men today."

I look at my mom, and I can see she is reliving the horror of her mother's amputations; she'd never left her side. I try to thank my mom, but my tongue is too thick from the morphine and I pass out in spite of the pain.

When I come to again my mother has vanished and I watch the big hand on the large wall clock slowly spin around; it chases the small hand past 10, 11, 12, 1. I am drifting in and out, and my ankle still feels like it's being beaten with a sledgehammer. At first I see the shadow of a man lifting the hammer over his head and pounding my ankle as if he were beating in a railroad tie: KA-WHAM! KA-WHAM! KA-WHAM! But then a dark, masked figure interrupts the beating when he opens the door and stalks dreamlike across the room to the bed next to me. Swathed in black, the masked man raises a knife over his head and is about to plunge it into the white sheets when a nurse the size of a small bear comes out of nowhere, grabs the knife, and throws the man to the floor. I remember hearing the double concussion of her fist hitting his face and his head slamming against the cold tile before she yells for security. Two armed guards storm into the room, handcuff the man, and drag him into the hallway.

"I told you he was going to come back and off me!" I hear someone scream. For the first time I realize there is someone in the bed next to me; Nurse Bear turns on the light. A young black man is lying there, tubes hanging out of his nose and arm. But that's all that registers before my heavy eyelids droop closed, and I see the shadow of a man pounding my ankle again: KA-WHAM! KA-WHAM! KA-WHAM!

I almost jump out of bed the following morning when I feel someone roll me over and rub my ass with a cold swab of alcohol. I look up and see that I'm about to be stabbed with a knife; when I focus my eyes, though, I catch the downward arch of a thick silver needle. "No, no more!" I yell, rolling back over. "It doesn't help."

"Are you sure, honey?"

"Just aspirin. Please. That's all I want."

The Demerol has done nothing for the pain; worse, it's given me terrible nightmares about men with knives and sledgehammers. I've also had bad feelings about what is going to happen to me once I got out of the hospital: if I need drugs for my ankle just lying in a hospital bed, what kind of junkie will I turn into when I start walking on it again?

But I needn't have worried about that. Later that morning the orthopod tells me I'll never use my ankle again.

"It'd be better if we amputated it," he says, holding an x-ray overhead. "With an injury like that, you won't be able to stand the pain. Besides, you'll never run or climb on that ankle again."

The throbbing pain has not abated, and he knows it. And he's obviously ready to wheel me back into surgery and fire up his bone saw. But the finality of an amputation is too depressing for me to consider—and I am not about to let anybody cut off my foot without seeing for myself just how bad it is.

"I'll see what I can do with it," I say, trying to hold back the tears as he plods out of the room.

His prognosis devastates me, but the day goes from bad to worse when I realize the man next to me is a gunshot victim; a dark red hole in his left thigh oozes pus and he assures me I wasn't having a nightmare about someone trying to murder him in his sleep. . . . But before he can finish laying on me the details of a nickel drug deal gone sour, my fiance, Anna, strides into the room pushing an empty wheelchair; saying little more than hello, she wheels me down the hallway into the empty waiting room where we can have some privacy. But just when I expect her to wrap her arms around me, and maul me with love, and tell me everything is going to be all right, she does a Jekyll-and-Hyde and starts screaming at me.

"Look what you've done to us! How are you going to make a living now? You're in a county hospital, and you can't even pay the bill! How are you going to take care of us? What am I going to tell my parents about the wedding, huh?"

When Anna wheels me back into my room, I feel like a broken man being sealed in a tomb. She storms out, her breasts bouncing to her footsteps. I lie there crying and try to take my mind off the pain by making conversation with the dude next to me. But all he wants now, thank you very much, are the pain pills the nurses are still trying to force-feed me. Life, as I've known it the last three and a half years, has ended. I haven't planned it that way, and I have no idea how I'm going to crawl out of the black hole I've fallen into.

III

When my mother wheels me out of the hospital a week later, I feel like somebody has slid open the lid on my crypt. I squint my eyes, then blink nervously trying to adjust to daylight again. But the sun is too bright, so I shade my eyes as she rolls me toward the car. I take in a deep breath; the faint whiff of orange blossoms is still in the air; and a chorus of birds is furiously singing in the spring. I am alive again—wobbly, but alive. And I have only one thing on my mind: climbing Squaw Peak. It was the only thing that had kept me from plunging farther into an abyss of despair during the long, tormented hours I lay trapped in the county hospital with an ankle that felt like it'd been used as an anvil.

But Anna wants nothing to do with my climbing Squaw Peak with my leg still in a cast, she tells me later that same day. "You're only going to hurt yourself worse!" she slams the door to my apartment and speeds out of the driveway.

I lie there alone on the couch wondering why I'd confided my deepest fears in her, my fear of being forced to give up the thing I loved most, the wilderness. If I can't use my foot, how am I going to climb mountains? How am I going to explore canyons and cross deserts? How am I going to teach again?

Maybe the doctor was right. Pain has been my constant companion since I took the fall. It's still there, alone with me under the sheets when I try to sleep; it mugs me when I crawl to the bathroom in the middle of the night; it's by my side when I try burying myself in reading. KA-WHAM! KA-WHAM! KA-WHAM! I can't shake it, no matter what I do. And I drag it around my small apartment as if the jaws of a pit bull were clamped on the end of my leg. So how much more painful could climbing Squaw Peak be, I wonder? At least I'd be outside, in the sunshine, trying to do something about my situation. And what was there to hurt, really? They already want to amputate my foot.

Still wracked with pain, weeks later I realize my whole life hinged on climbing the mountain. Because the future never looked bleaker. I was stone broke, I was about to be evicted from my apartment, and I had no way to make a living unless I could somehow teach the backpacking and wilderness survival course that had been postponed while I was in the hospital. But if I could somehow climb the mountain, I know in my heart I'll be able to teach again. But without teaching, I'll have to take handouts, and I am too proud for that. And without my ankle I can't teach. As the walls of my apartment slowly close in on me, and as the pain continues to hammer and chew away at me, I realize teaching has become my life and my livelihood.

What had started out as a modest proposal to Dean Larry Stevens, that Scottsdale Community College offer a few outdoor courses, had, without my planning, caught the crest of the backpacking wave. And after one marginally successful test course—and a flurry of press releases hammered out by the college's master of P.R.—I found that I had unknowingly stumbled into a full-time profession. At the time, however, I was already a full-time drama student at the college, living hand-to-mouth, as most struggling actors do, taking any low-end job that offered a meal and a paycheck. But that was nothing new. Since the time of Shakespeare in Elizabethan England, aspiring actors have been treated as though they were the scourge of society; and unless you were a trust-fund baby, being a drama student in a pretentious resort town like Scottsdale was only one notch above being a leper. No one was going to offer a high paying job to a struggling actor who was preoccupied with memorizing lines, building sets, or rehearsing six weeks at a crack. So the sudden opportunity to earn enough money as a teacher, to move my sleeping bag out of a photographer friend's claustrophobic, dektol-drenched darkroom, was too good to pass up.

But I soon learned I had taken on more than I could handle by myself. To my surprise, more people stood in line to register for the courses I was teaching than to see the plays I acted in. So I was faced with the dilemma of squeezing more and more students into a single class or offering another course the following month to accommodate the overflow, and another course after that to accommodate the overflow from the second course, until the whole thing snowballed.

That's when Tony and Randy Mulkey entered my life. Like me, they were both drama majors and they both had a passion for the wilderness. They'd also proven themselves as students and as reliable field assistants in the first courses I taught, and I had come to depend on them both. The core Backpacking & Wilderness Survival course being offered, however, wasn't exactly a walk in the park; as modest as my paychecks were, I didn't feel anybody needed to pay me good money to show them how to feed the ducks. Spun out over four weekends, interspersed with exhausting midweek lectures sandwiched between play rehearsals, each course was designed to build confidence in all students, so that by the time they finished they'd have a solid background in wilderness travel and survival. The best way to do that, I found, was to let Arizona's wild landscape impart its own lessons and lasting impressions: first by leading them across remote desert ranges, then by tackling Arizona's highest mountains, the 12,633-foot-high San Francisco Mountains, and finally by descending into the depths of the Grand Canyon along some little-known route. Tony and Randy, together with another friend named Gary Drysmala, provided the safety net I thought was needed for students to explore some of the most awe-inspiring terrain in the Southwest.

But even with soulmates like them to rely on, the strain of constantly making sure a student never got injured was taking its toll on me. The more I taught, the less I climbed for myself. And after a successful three-and-a-half year run of back-to-back courses, I became increasingly aware that if I were ever to fulfill my own burning ambition to climb in the Himalayas I would have to test myself outside the arena of an instructor who'd long since memorized every move on every rock climb he'd ever led a student up. Then, that's what had led to my fall.

Held hostage by pain in my own apartment, there was little else to distract me other than analyzing the events leading up to my fall. It wasn't the difficulty of the route; on Granite Mountain the same move would have protected and the same handhold would have held the weight of a truck. It was simply fatigue and rotten rock. Stretched out on the couch, tossing and turning from pain, I knew I couldn't change the past. But somehow I had to come to grips with the present and with how I was going to survive the future. I was convinced I had to climb the mountain to see whether the journey would provide any solutions.

Fortunately, Tony understood, because about the time I was ready to knock out the walls of my apartment with my crutches, he gave me a ride to Squaw Peak.

"When do you want me to come back and get you?" he asked.

"Late this afternoon," I said.

"Sure you don't want me to go with?"

"This is something I gotta' do alone, Tone."

"I know."

Squaw Peak stands as the bold, pyramidal high point of the Phoenix Mountains, which, at one time, was roamed by members of the ancient Hohokam culture; they settled in the Salt River Valley about A.D. 1000 and, no doubt, made the first ascent of the 2,608-foot mountain to harvest saguaro fruit long before Spanish missionary Padre Eusebio Kino first ventured into the *Valle del Sol* on March 2, 1699. A few centuries later, a rough miner's trail was hacked into the side of the mountain to reach a "gloryhole" dynamited into a small notch below the summit. But long after those diggings went bust, Valley residents began making daily pilgrimages up the mountain, both for their health and as a way of fleeing the stranglehold of development that now encircles this Sonoran desert mountain range.

For my students, though, Squaw Peak was both a testing place and a training ground en route to more remote and challenging terrain. Yet for many it remained an enthralling climb in itself; in another time and another place, Squaw Peak could easily be mistaken for a mountain of daunting proportions. It is dark, angular, and brooding, yet it is always magnetic, beckoning all who approach it.

As I crutch up the first switchback, short of breath, I know the craggy summit of Squaw Peak is far beyond my reach today; so I resign myself to seeing how far I can get before turning back. I plant both crutches on the rocky trail in front of me, swing my right leg out front, and plant it squarely on the hard ground like the third leg of a tripod; that done, I swing my heavy plaster cast up beside my right leg and hold it in midair as I swing my crutches out front again. I plant my right foot again and swing my heavy cast. Each time I do, blood rushes to the bottom of my left foot and my ankle feels like a great throbbing toothache. But the pain is manageable, so long as I don't put any weight on the foot. And as long as the trail remains smooth and flat, it's like crutching up a sidewalk.

Gouged into the steep, rugged flanks of this desert peak, the trail climbs twelve hundred vertical feet in a little over a mile; to do that, it angles steeply, frequently zigzagging back and forth on itself like a series of Z's stacked atop one another. As soon as I hit the first steep switchbacks, my rhythmic crutching ends and my progress slows to a crawl. I stop, put my crutches to one side, ease into a sitting position, and stick my left leg out in front of me across the trail. I lean back against a warm rock and try to catch my breath as people walk around me. Recovered, I get up and tackle the next series of switchbacks with as much momentum as I can muster, before fatigue, throbbing pain, and shortness of breath force me to sit down and rest again. Fearing someone might step on my outstretched leg, I get up when the trail is clear of hikers, and I start the battle all over again.

I am sweating profusely, just as I had when my last class climbed out of the Grand Canyon; but unlike the elation of climbing out of the Canyon, I become wearier and more irritable the higher I crutch up the mountain. The cast is chafing the inside of my right leg, and my left thigh is on fire from carrying the heavy cast. But I crutch on, a switchback at a time, locked into my own miserable little struggle. I am so far removed from the person who ran up and down this trail a few weeks ago, I decide I can't go any farther; I sit down to catch my breath before heading back down the mountain to lick my wounds and tend to my bruised ego. Maybe the doctor was right, I think, but before I can get lost in self-pity a voice calls out, "Are you all right? Can I help?"

"I'm fine, thanks," I say gruffly, as if help is a personal affront to my character and abilities.

"Are you sure?"

"I said *no!*"

The woman strides past, and suddenly the warmth and kindness of her words sink in; they encourage me. I get up again and crutch up the next couple of switchbacks, chastising myself for being so rude to a stranger who'd offered to help a gimp like me. "What a jerk," I tell myself.

The last switchback tops out on a small vista and I use it as an excuse to sit down and rest. A warm breeze fans my sweat-soaked T-shirt. To the north, I can see the trail snaking its way along a serrated ridge line; I can rest on that stretch, I muse, before it climbs again, wrestle the next set of switchbacks, catch my breath again, then crawl the last quarter-mile if I have to. I ache all over from weeks of inactivity and my foot feels like it's going to explode, but for the first time I can actually see the summit. The thought of somehow reaching it, after weeks of languishing in an emotional dungeon, makes my heart soar.

Staring at the hard ground I've yet to cross, my thoughts drift back to Slavomir Rawicz's *The Long Walk*. It was required reading for all my students, and after my fall I repeatedly sought inspiration from the book throughout my couchbound internment. In 1941, seven political prisoners escaped from a grim Siberian slave camp near the Arctic Circle. In an adventure of truly epic proportions, they fled south across Mongolia, traversed the Gobi Desert, and crossed the Himalayas before reaching India and freedom, nine months and over 4,000 miles later. The trail ahead of me was nothing compared to their incredible journey. And my own suffering, as painful and as emotionally debilitating as it had been for me, was nothing compared to what that heroic band of men and one woman endured for months on end in their quest for freedom. Yes, I knew about wilderness travel and survival, but I knew nothing about suffering or endurance on that scale. If I ever wanted to use my ankle again, if I ever wanted to explore the frontiers of my own world, I would have to learn the art of suffering and endurance as they had. I would have to crawl before I walked again, and when I stumbled I'd have to crawl again; and I'd certainly have to walk before I could ever run. I had to start somewhere, and, at that moment, reaching the summit was my answer.

I struggle to my feet and start crutching my way up the mountain again. The pain is still there; it hasn't diminished for a moment since the fall and I don't know if it ever will. I try to detach myself from it, I try to embrace it, I curse it viciously, but it never relents; it dogs me every step of the way as I continue crutching toward the summit. If I am going to cross the threshold back to what I could do before my fall, pain, I now realize, will be the price of admission.

I crutch on throughout the afternoon, slowly, methodically, one switchback at a time, until I reach the summit cap. A scramble from the end of the trail up a short, chimneylike gully will put you, if you're whole, on top of the mountain. For me, it is the most dreadful stretch of rock I would ever climb. My right leg has been chafed raw by the cast. My left leg feels as if someone has doused it with gasoline and set it on fire. My ankle is being beaten and chewed by invisible demons. My armpits feel like they've been sandpapered. And my hands are numb from being locked, clawlike, around the wooden handles of my crutches. I put both crutches in front of me, hop up, and grab the black rock with one hand. I push the crutches up the rock overhead and, reluctantly, let go of them. I grab the rock with both hands, stand squarely on the toes of my right foot, and hold my left leg out in the air. I hop up the next little foothold. I push my crutches up again and grab the next handhold, one hand at a time, and hop up again. I repeat this awkward, painful process until I can't go up any farther. Suddenly, I can see over the other side; I am on the summit.

I stand up with my crutches and sway in the wind with exhaustion. Tears are streaming down my swollen cheeks. Salt stings my eyes and sunburned lips, but I am on top of the world. The Valley is spread out far below. Mountains I'd climbed and trekked with my students can be seen in every direction. I've made it!

CHAPTER TWO

Running Wild

From the Superstition mountain rose the Eagle;
From the sluggish-moving Gila rose the Hawk . . .
There I am running, there I am running.
The Shadow of Crooked Mountain.

Pima Legend

"I slept with Ronnie; I want a divorce."

For months, the words had echoed through my head as I ran alone through the desert night. They'd chase me like demons, haunting me with anguish. But tonight, still running alone in the shadow of the heavens, they finally mean nothing; they float away in space, as empty and meaningless as the lifelong promise Anna made to me when she said, *I do* or when the doctor said *you'll never run . . . again.*

Stars flicker brilliantly as I run deeper into the dark night below; I swing my arms in rhythmic union with my breathing and periodically adjust my footsteps to the surface of the dirt pathway underfoot. Somewhere high above, a great horned owl hoots at my approach, but I can see nothing but the faint, stark outlines of cottonwood trees as I stride past; they are enormous, cauliflower-shaped black shadows backlit against the dark horizon by distant lights of earthen dwellings still inhabited by Native Americans. For generations, these peaceful Pima and Maricopa inhabited a

vast ancestral land, which, in 1700, still comprised most of
the central Arizona desert surrounding the Salt and Gila
rivers. About that time, the fleet-footed Maricopa traveled
to the far ends of their territory and beyond during week-
long, 250-mile runs to the Colorado River Delta in order to
trade for tobacco with the Cocopas, as if they were going to
the store for a pack of smokes. But that was long before the
white man tortured, subdued, and corralled them like live-
stock on a small reservation with the Pima, a reservation
now bordered by the upscale Anglo community of Scottsdale. ("The home of fifty-cent millionaires," a crotchety old
real estate instructor told us in class one night.) The dichotomy between these two communities was as striking as that
between most prosperous American border towns and their
desperate "neighbors" to the south. The difference was that
the Pima and Maricopa didn't lust for the life of the affluent
city dwellers to the west; like many Native Americans, their
hearts longed to roam freely across their ancestral lands.
What little of it was parceled out to them in the form of the
Salt River Indian Reservation had become their refuge from
a foreign culture that turned their traditional life and spiritways inside out.

Admittedly I was an uninvited guest, but the sparse
lands of Pima and Maricopa also became my own refuge,
albeit a transient one. But I wanted nothing from these Native Americans I could take away from them; I wouldn't
make them promises I wouldn't keep; I didn't even want
them to see me, lest they rightfully ban me from their un-
hurried land. I wanted only to run alone, sight unseen, at
night, on the edge of a world that had also caused me so
much pain. It was out here that I learned to distance myself
from heart-shattering words and emotions and from the
power they held over my life in the other world beyond the
reservation line; it was here that I replayed images from that

life on a celestial screen that extended from one horizon to the next and as far back into my past as I dared delve; it was here, in the land of the Pima and Maricopa, that I learned to run again.

My feet continue padding softly along the dirt path, sending up powdery wisps of dust with each footfall. I suck wind in, I blow air out: *hih-huh, hih-huh, hih-huh, hih-huh*. My lungs heave in and out, charged by my swinging arms. Frogs croak from the narrow irrigation ditch beside me. The whistling scream of nighthawks can be heard as they swoop down and snatch insects buzzing above the irrigated fields surrounding me. Only occasionally do I feel a painful twinge in my ankle. My strides are full, flowing, as if I can't run fast enough tonight.

But it wasn't always like that, even on reservation land. One of the first nights I ran out here I chased a coyote— God's Dog, Native Americans sometimes called it, The Trickster. Only this coyote was white, a pale white with faint buff-colored markings, but white. It loped out of deep cotton, where it had been lying in wait for dinner. The sun had just gone down, and I was running east toward Crooked Mountain when I almost collided with it. Instead of sprinting away from me, though, it loped defiantly in front of me, just out of reach, as I tried to catch up with it. I distinctly remember it looking back over its shoulder at me, playfully mouthing the lifeless clump of a bloody white-wing dove; it seemed to laugh at me as I limped after it, my leg sometimes buckling from the pain as I ran harder to catch it. But just as I would start to close the gap, it would trot ahead again, just out of reach, and start its game of catch-me-if-you-can all over again. When the coyote finally grew bored, it loped off the trail and became a blurred flash of white burning through the creosote flats, running as effortlessly as a desert wind. In contrast, I limped like a wounded animal several miles back to the college parking lot, my right leg carrying the burden of my left as I learned to do those painfully slow and difficult first miles. I had to tell Gary what I'd seen.

"Are you sure it was white?" Gary asked, lighting the acetylene torch with the flick of his flint starter; he was at the college working on a new piece of metal sculpture, and I thought his artistic sensibilities might accept the image of a white coyote without too great a leap of faith.

"I'm sure it was white; I've never seen anything like it before," I said, almost pleading with him to believe me.

Gary swept back his long, brown hair, pulled down his dark welder's goggles, and grinned, silently toying with the image in his mind.

But I *hadn't* seen anything like it before. That's why I continued to run on the reservation at twilight. I wanted to know if what I'd seen was real, or if it was a visual distortion caused by pain and exhaustion. When fever-struck prospectors trekked sixty miles down Kanab Creek in the 1870s for the gold rumored to be near its confluence with the Colorado River, many dropped out from hunger and sheer exhaustion; others pushed on into the western Grand Canyon, as one historian wrote, "determined to 'see the elephant' for themselves after so long and fatiguing a journey." After a while, I began wondering if I'd "seen the elephant," because as much as I ran after and searched for *coyote blanco,* I never saw it again. What I did see in pursuit of it was pain, every shade of it. But with it came the growing realization that my ankle was slowly getting better and that I could actually run on it again without limping or crying.

But it hadn't started out that way.

Not long after I crawled down Squaw Peak, Anna and I were married. I remember crutching up the sidewalk to the altar when one of my students grabbed the sleeve of my coat. Rex Woods was a bartender at a Scottsdale resort, and

his wit was honed from years of verbal jousting with bab-
bling snowbirds—Arizona's winter visitors. Standing there
in the sunlight, he looked me in the eye and, only half
jokingly, said, "John, it's not too late; I've got the car running." I should have listened. When I crutched up to the
stagelike altar Anna had prepared, I watched, along with
several hundred embarrassed guests at the outdoor ceremony, as Anna tried to set two white doves free. On the
verge of hysteria, she frantically shook the flowered cage.
The frightened doves wouldn't budge, and the image of our
love remained frozen there. That was my second opportunity to bail out. The third time came when Anna's father
marched—in front of God, my parents, everyone—to the
podium and harangued the crowd like a Third World dicta-
tor; he told us all exactly what he thought of Anna and me
getting married. Two and a half years later he got his wish;
his daughter's little adventure was over, and my heart was
broken.

I was eighteen days into a 750-mile wilderness trek
across Arizona when Anna broke the news to me, and it
literally stopped me in my tracks.

After crawling, crying, and hobbling around on a
tender ankle for two years in preparation for the adventure,
I knew the only way to prove my ankle could stand the
rigors of resuming a full-time career in outdoor education
would be to trek the length of Arizona from the Mexican
border to the Utah state line. I started planning for the trip
the year Anna and I spent in Prescott, where I was both a
student and a part-time outdoor instructor at Prescott College. Crossing the state on foot meant no less to me than had
climbing Squaw Peak; I also felt our marriage sorely needed
it, because without full use of my ankle I often felt like only
half a man. But this was no afternoon crawl up a desert
peak; it was a two-month trek across some of the most
rugged and beautiful terrain in the Southwest, and I'd have

to train hard for it. The pine-clad mountains of mile-high Prescott were perfect for that. And when, degree in hand, I moved back to the Valley with Anna, I concentrated much of my energy on training for the Arizona crossing. The reservation was the only place I ran, and the more I ran the better my ankle got. Even the doctor expressed disbelief when viewing the x-rays: "I thought the talus would have died by now." The bone hadn't died, as he'd feared, but it was still painful to put in my daily ten miles in preparation for the trek.

And as the departure date drew nearer, I started having doubts about whether I was doing the right thing, or whether I was going to fail miserably, as Anna's father predicted I would. However, barely a week north of Mexico, all my fears were dispelled. Carrying a heavy pack was still painful, but after a few hours of trekking my ankle would warm to the occasion . . . and as one day faded into the next, the ankle quickly grew stronger, and Jack Cartier and I kept bearing northwest from the Chiricahua Mountains, across the Galiuro Wilderness, and into Aravaipa Canyon. While hopping over a log there, Jack wrenched his knee and reluctantly fell back into vehicle support position as I continued to trek north.

A few days north of Aravaipa, however, I had Jack give me a ride to a phone. I wanted to give Anna a quick progress report before I tackled the Superstition Wilderness. I hadn't seen her for more than two weeks, and I was excited to tell her my ankle was holding together. At last, we could have a new life together, free from the pain and uncertainty that had shadowed us since our marriage. I picked up the phone and dialed.

"Anna," I said, as soon as I heard her pick up the phone on the other end, "I love you." There was a long silence; maybe we had a bad connection. So I said it again. "Anna, I love you." Then with no warning whatsoever, without a clue in the world on my part, she said, "I slept with Ronnie. I want a divorce."

I was stunned. I felt like I'd been kicked in the stomach, then hit across the back of my head with a bat. For the second time in two years my world came crashing down on me, and I was stopped cold in my tracks. I quit. I felt like dying.

When I returned to the Valley, I sought relief from my pain by running long hours through the land of the Pima and Maricopa. At first I wanted to flee Arizona altogether, maybe hole up in Telluride, Colorado; I had had a small climbing school there a few years earlier, and I couldn't think of a better place to lick my wounds than in the snow-capped Rockies, far removed from the harsh realities of the desert below. But if my ankle had taught me nothing else, it had taught me that if I started running away from the pain I'd be a transient prisoner of a broken heart, and life was just too short for that. I'd have to deal with the terrible pain of my divorce day in and day out, the same way I had learned to endure the pain in my ankle. The best way to do that, I decided, was to get a job with Anna's father, selling cars, where I'd be forced to confront my emotions head on. Oddly enough, Anna's father actually gave me a job at one of his five car dealerships. Partly, I suspected, because he would relish the thought of my failing; it would prove to Anna beyond a doubt that I never deserved to marry into a family whose wealth was estimated at $20 million. Maybe the whole marriage had tainted me, but after two years of Anna's family treating me like a crippled low-life artist who supported his acting habit by teaching outdoor education, of all things, I began wondering whether I could make it in the "real world." So I sold cars, small foreign jobs at a glass-shrouded car palace.

However, if I was once led to believe there was fast, easy money to be made on a car lot, it didn't take me long to realize that gonzo journalist Hunter S. Thompson was right when he wrote, "We're a nation of used car salesmen." Everybody who walked onto that car lot wanted to sell me his used car retail and buy his new car wholesale. It was human nature, and trust never entered the picture; the only thing that mattered was who offered the best deal in town. Still, the customers always fascinated me. What interested them about life? What were their passions? Professions? I wanted to know. If the make of the car was really any good, and they really wanted it, the situation would sell itself. If not, at least I had learned something about their characters. And, for someone schooled in drama, learning the dynamics behind a character was everything.

But even with daily character studies to take my mind off the divorce and its cruel finality, there were some days I felt just plain weird working at a car lot, dressed like a poor pimp, and for my ex's father, of all people. Fortunately, I had a safety net by the name of Mike Johnson. "Hot Deals" Johnson, Randy and I used to call him at play rehearsals, because he was always coming up with some new bizarre tale or an idea that came from so far out in left field you wouldn't have believed him unless he walked the Abominable Snowman into your living room on a chain. Like Randy and me, Johnson also envisioned himself on the silver screen with a face and head the size of a hot air balloon. So selling cars suited him perfectly until Hollywood called. But it was the phrases Johnson coined that made me realize I didn't need to be buried by the depression of a divorce or even the strangeness of the situation; in Johnson's eyes, we were just playing another part, on a different stage, and he matched the names to each new scene. "Taillight Guarantee" for instance, meant a used car was guaranteed to run until the salesman could no longer see its taillights once the customer drove it off the lot. "Slurpees" usually came in couples; they visited the car lot only on Friday nights after slamming their way through happy hour, and the guy always tried to impress his date by having her sit behind the wheel of the most expensive car on the showroom floor and then, fingering his wallet, asking "How much if I pay cash?" But Slurpees, as Johnson was quick to point out, not only never paid cash, they rarely signed a contract. "Leakers" pissed away your time, and "Strokers" never bought a car, not at any price. Schooled and entertained by Johnson, my sales the first month mounted until I was vying for Salesman of the Month with Hot Deals himself. But I was giving away my commissions to do it.

Thereafter, for a reluctant car salesman, my life at the time was ascetically simple. I divided it between the car lot, running at night on the reservation, and trying to sleep through the stifling spring heat in the air-conditionerless trailer I shared with Randy. But slowly the pain of my divorce subsided, along with that in my ankle. And when the turbulent emotions I felt toward Anna, her father, and myself had finally been stilled by long, soothing hours of running, when an internal calm once again prevailed, I knew it was time to say good-bye to Johnson, Randy, Tony, and Gary, the friendships we shared. Johnson was going to Hollywood to seek fame and fortune in the movie business; Randy would join the pilgrimage to Tinseltown as soon as he got his S.A.G. (Screen Actor's Guild) card; Tony was fleeing to Flagstaff to build a house in the pines; Gary was headed to New Mexico to open up a studio; and I was moving to Prescott to write the novel I wanted to star in. But before I did, I wanted to take a final run on the reservation.

That's where I was now.

The road tunneled its way toward the full moon rising in the east, and I ran toward it with all my heart. My footsteps were pounding effortlessly, my arms were swinging with streamlined efficiency, breathing came as easy as if pumped by simoom winds. There was no pain, anywhere. At last I was free, and my path led straight into the craters of the moon, which now hung suspended over the forbidding Superstition Mountains. I longed to visit them again; the last time I had, I was leading a charge of students from the back of a stable horse when the cinch on my saddle broke; I was dumped on the hard desert floor, helpless with my leg still encased in plaster. Those days were gone now, and as I ran I could see the future stretched out before me, unbound by torment and pain. Linked only by my footsteps which continued to leave their faint marks on the desert floor. I hoped to visit those mountains again, as the ancient Pima had when they sang: "From the Superstition Mountain rose the Eagle; From the sluggish-moving Gila rose the Hawk . . . There I am running; there I am running. The shadow of Crooked Mountain." I wanted to visit Crooked Mountain again, running wild as I was now through the heart of the moon.

II

Seven months later I run out of the other side of that desert moon, a slipstream of diaphanous images whirling in my wake. I've emerged from the desert floor of the Pima and Maricopa and am now running through the ancient mountain sanctuary of the Yavapai people, a world dominated by huge granite boulders and crystal-blue skies airbrushed with the pine-green scent of swaying ponderosa pines.

It is January. A cool winter sun is crawling out of the horizon, slowly burning the thin layer of frost off the path in front of me as I run deeper into the Granite Mountain massif. Dense clusters of pinyon and juniper trees mask the horizon immediately to the north, and prickly pear cactus shower my bare legs with hundreds of tiny arrowlike glochids as I brush past. I tear over a small rise, kicking up small roostertails of dust and dirt behind me. I suck in deep drafts of bitingly cold mountain air and fly down the other side of the hill, flapping my arms in hopes of slowing my descent. But it is too late. My feet slide hopelessly on the decomposed granite surface, a thousand ball bearings of coarse stone catapulting me toward a bone-rattling wreck. I tumble out of control and soar through the air as if I've fallen from the back of a speeding pickup. Fortunately, I land in a sandy wash wound around the bottom of the hill like a lazy snake and the impact is not as punishing as I expect it to be. WHHOOSSHH! Sand explodes everywhere. I spit cold damp sand out of my mouth and spray the ground in front of me with stringy egg whites of mucous and sand as I blow out each nostril. I brush sand off my face and shake it out of my hair. But suddenly, I hear a chorus of ugly grunting. I jump to my feet and see that I'm sur-rounded by a leaderless band of saber-tusked peccaries run-ning blindly around me without a clue in the world as to what caused the stampede. Javelina, a dozen or more of them brandishing razor-sharp incisors as long as my little fingers, root up the ground around me with small, black, cloven hooves, grunting: *huug, huug, huug, huug, huug.* I stand there breathless, looking for the nearest tree to climb before these near-blind desert "pigs" find me and strip my bare legs of flesh with the same carnivorous fervor I experi-ence when gnawing on greasy barbecued ribs. But there is nowhere to run and nowhere to climb; I stand there, scarecrowlike, knowing that any animal that relishes eating the needle-covered pads of prickly pear cactus would have no problem munching on my spindly legs.

Fortunately, they don't see me. The pack of small bearlike peccaries resumes its noisy foraging along the dry wash as I resume running toward Granite Mountain Saddle, trying to shake out the imminent bruises. At one time, Granite Mountain lay within the vast ancestral lands of the

Yavapai. Like many Native Americans in the Southwest, the Yavapai were fleet of foot; during June they were known to make an arduous journey from the vicinity of Prescott into the appalling summer heat of the Sonoran desert to the south in order to collect saguaro fruit. In early autumn, they'd return to Granite Mountain to harvest juniper berries, which still grow profusely in the area, as well as walnuts, acorns, and even the manzanita berries that adorn a slick-red-barked bush many Anglos now like to spray paint silver and use for Christmas decorations. No doubt the Yavapai's foraging trips into this basin were more than that; perhaps they were inextricably linked with their spiritways, since one archaeologist wrote that Yavapai spirits "were said to inhabit Granite Peak."

Running toward Granite Mountain Saddle, wearing little more than a pair of shorts and a wool sweater to insulate myself from the elements, I find it easy to understand the power and sanctity the area held for the Yavapai; they also used the mountain as a natural granite fortress in which to elude white men who hunted them like dogs during the 1870s. Even famed "Indian tracker" Al Sieber was quick to admit the frustration of trying to track the Yavapai in a place like Granite Mountain, because it entailed "scores of miles of the most backbreaking travel, and if any sign at all was uncovered, you were lucky, so elusive was the enemy. It was discouraging." Fortunately.

Were it not for the modern trail hacked out of brush and blasted out of hard rock, my running through this stony domain would be discouraging too, but I didn't come to disturb the Yavapai spirits that may dwell in a region now fenced and labeled by Anglos as wilderness, only to glimpse this mountain the way it might once have been seen by a native people who lived in harmony with it, who unlike the white man, did not view it as wild. I adjust my stride, my breathing, to the gradient of this well-trod trail as it climbs higher out of the headwaters of Granite Creek toward the saddle high above.

Built during the Depression by homeless men using black powder and hard metal tools, the trail I'm running up bears little resemblance to the ancient footpaths early Yavapai people etched here with ceaseless footsteps during their nomadic wanderings, which sometimes led them from the snow-dusted Bradshaw Mountains into the sun-scorched deserts of western Arizona. No other tribe in Arizona thrived, as the Yavapai reputedly could, in such a diverse spectrum of life zones, or biological communities. One can only assume that they ran in order to cover great distances across an ancestral region that once encompassed 20,000 square miles, just as other Southwest peoples had; the Mojave, the Chemehuevi, the Hopi, the Paiute, and the Tohono O'odham are but a few of the native peoples historians tell us could run upwards of a hundred miles in a day, day after day, easier than I now am as these handtooled switchbacks grow steeper and the pain of the ascent becomes more evident.

My lungs burn from the altitude and my throat feels red and raw from the cold. I pump my arms harder, but my thighs, covered with a thin sheen of cold sweat, also burn from the steep climb. I shake my gloveless fingers as I run, then blow on them; they too have grown stiff and numb with cold as I pass beneath the huge rock wall of Granite Mountain. I try to warm myself in the brittle morning air by running faster. Only momentarily are my thoughts drawn to the wall's cracks, chimneys, and faces, which provided me and other climbers with hours of gritty climbing during the pleasant Indian summer days of fall. Why Tony and I hadn't come to climb this immaculate shield of rock instead of that Phoenix slagheap is only a flicker of a thought before it vanishes. I crest the cold, windswept summit of Granite Mountain Saddle, panting dragonlike puffs of hot moist air.

Wind-hardened snow blankets the saddle like an ice-cap, and a north wind whistles south through the pines, promising stone-cold feet if I venture beyond. My immediate thought is to flee back the way I came. I know the route now. It is safe. It is certain. It is also downhill. I'd only have to wait a couple of hours for Chris to pick me up, once she realized I hadn't gone over the saddle to our scheduled rendezvous on the other side of the mountain. I peer over the north side of the saddle; if I'd enjoyed the visceral warmth of the winter sun on the south side of the saddle, it looks bleak, snowy, and dangerous to the north. Worse, I can't find the trail indicated on the topographical map I'm clutching in my cold hands. Still, I'm tempted to see what's on the other side, if only because this is the first time I've attempted to traverse a mountain by running it; I won't have any idea how Southwest Native Americans ran across mountains unless I find out—the hard way. The twelve hundred miles I have run since moving to Prescott, trying to adapt to the rigors of altitude, hills, and trails, have led me to this point. I know what is behind me; curiosity and the unknown push me over the edge, and I have no idea what lies beyond.

I plunge downward, but I immediately begin post-holing in the crusty snow with all the finesse of a bawling calf caught in a deep snowdrift. The steep descent and sheer gravity carry me downward as I slalom through the black-barked trees like a man being hunted. The sharp crust of snow scrapes my bare legs as they perforate the crust, but the depth and compactness of the snow isn't enough to slow my descent. My speed increases. I grab wildly at the branches of small pines, but they are cold and wet and their slick green needles slide out of my hands like tiny frozen fish. My momentum snowballs, until I am no longer post-holing but sliding downward atop the ice-encrusted snow. I plop down on my backside before I crash headlong against a tree. I put my feet out in front of me to break my descent, but the soft rubber heels of my shoes won't bite into the hard crust and for the second time today I careen toward destruction. Now desperate, I swing around and slide head-first on my stomach toward a small pine tree in hopes of tackling it before I fly off the abrupt drop that looms ahead. WHACK! My tackle holds for a moment as I take the brunt of the impact across my right collar bone, but the momentum of my legs swinging across the steep ice in a wide arc jerks me loose and the bark-covered leg of the pine tree slips out of my grasp; suddenly, I'm avalanching toward the drop again. I flail widely at anything and everything, as if I'm clawing at a torn football jersey in hopes of saving the tackle, and a lone branch tears and burns through my right hand until a cluster of pine needles anchors itself in my palm; it stops me in a spray of ice.

My slushy wet feet skate wildly on the ice as I scurry back up to the small tree, but I manage to wrestle around it until I'm on the uphill side of it again. This puny pine is all that stands between me and the drop below; a drop, I now see, over a granite step that would have ended in broken bones, blood, and ice. Before cold completely overcomes me, I quickly plot my course around this drop, and around a half-dozen other backbreakers lurking below, and pick out a small ridgeline leading down into Williamson Valley. I post-hole over to it in thigh-deep snow; the crusty stranglehold at the bottom of each step tries to wrench off my icy shoes, but I've knotted my laces for the worst and when I finally reach the ridgeline, still wearing both shoes, I'm breathing like a sled dog.

My feet are cold, almost numb. So I run downhill through the snow with wild abandon, frequently plowing through deep drifts as fast as I can in hopes of restoring circulation; when it finally returns, I break out of the trees like a dream run amok.

"Annerino, over here!" I hear a voice in the distance

crying out. It's Chris Keith, my roommate, and today, my shuttle driver. I've survived, not with much grace, but the ensuing adrenalin rush only boils my blood to run wild again.

The next time I do, I'm running alone through the Galiuro Mountains. It's a cool, clear day in March; a brisk wind rustles out of the north. My legs feel strong, and I feel confident I can run fifty miles across the mountain island in a day. That's only half the distance the Apaches reportedly ran between sunup and sunset through these parts; then, that's what's lured me to this isolated tract of southeastern Arizona to begin with—the idea of running, as I now am, carrying little more than a knife, flint and steel, some rations.

I suck wind in, I blow air out: *hih-huh, hih-huh, hih-huh, hih-huh*. My lungs heave in and out, my legs charge toward the power I hunger for, "running power." Apaches called it *galke?ho?ndi*. Keith Basso described it in *Western Apache Raiding & Warfare*: "A man who has this power can run long distances, and even on the shortest day could run from Fort Grant to Fort Apache and get there in mid-afternoon."

An 1881 military map from the Court Martial Case Files, on record at the National Archives, shows this Indian trail: by way of the crow, it's eighty miles from the north end of the Galiuro Mountains to the foot of the White Mountains; throw in the endless twists and turns of the rugged topography in between and you're looking at a hundred miles. In a day. A hundred miles in a day! What was it like for the Apache to run that? No one knows for certain. Native Americans have a great oral tradition of recording events and tribal history, so one can only speculate on what they thought about, or what it actually felt like to run a hundred miles wearing little more than a pair of leather moccasins, or straw sandals, and a traditional breech cloth.

The one known case documenting such a run concerns the remarkable escape of two Apache women circa 1865. Shanghaied by government troops, the women broke out of a military garrison in Tucson and ran more than 170 miles back to their village near Goodwin Springs, surviving on roasted mescal stalks along the way. But the single, most telling piece of evidence from the account in Basso's book came at the end of that extraordinary run when one of the women was later recognized by one of her original captors. According to Basso's principal informant, David Longstreet, "the officer shook hands with her." Longstreet added, "He wanted to know how she got home. She told him her legs were like horses!"

That's how my legs still felt ten miles into the Galiuros, which some early travelers named the Sierra del Arivaya for the creek they followed north between the Galiuro and Pinaleño mountains. Averaging 250 miles of running a month since Granite Mountain, I had few worries, other than fatigue, about trying to bite off half the distance the Apache historically ran in a day. Four miles later, however, my legs are seized with cramps, as if they've been painfully trussed in the same kind of air splint I wore after my fall. I walk peg leg-like for a few minutes and guzzle a liter of water from one of the two bota bags I'm wearing crisscrossed across my chest, Pancho Villa style. I cinch down my camera to my survival belt and start running again, trying to shake out the rigid cramps with a flick at each step, as if I'm practicing a military drill.

But the trail I'm running up, stiff-legged, is covered with fallen trees called blowdown, and to make any progress at all I have to crawl under or climb over them. The gymnastic moves, however, combined with the abrupt ascent, exhaust me by the time I finally reach the East Divide seventeen miles out. My thighs are screaming and my eyelids are starting to droop. I am totally spent. I can't go any farther. I should turn back, it's all downhill. But I can't; I've been dropped off on the southern end of one of the most remote and seldom-visited wilderness areas in the Southwest.

Sitting alone atop the Galiuros, halfway between hell and gone, I can see Eagle Pass between the Santa Teresa and Pinaleño mountains; the Spaniards used that pass when they called the Galiuros the Sierra de San Calistro. But I quickly lose that train of thought because I feel weak, unnaturally so. I must have a low-grade infection. My face feels flushed and the recovery I'm patiently waiting for never materializes. I look at my maps; I have no options. The shortest distance to any kind of help is to my rendezvous point at Power's Garden sixteen miles North. Somehow I have to make it there by nightfall. I'm not carrying any kind of sleeping gear and it's too cold to spend the night in the open. Sick or not, somehow I have to run it; I'm too lightly clad to move any slower.

I stand up, stretch my legs, and start running due north along the highline spine of the Galiuro Mountains, an unforgivingly rugged, 76,317-acre wilderness area. In terms of natural direction finding, I visualize this 7,000-foot mountain range in my mind's eye as a capital H lying on its backside. I am running along the lower right leg of that H, and somehow I have to reach Power's Garden, situated in a deep cleft of a canyon between the two upper arms of the H. But the slippery, narrow path I'm following is heavily overgrown with manzanita bushes, which shove me back and forth across the ridgeline like an unruly mob. Consequently, it takes all my concentration to maintain a run.

Feeling weaker by the yard, I'm not sure how much longer I can maintain this awkward, simian lurching, so I try daydreaming about the climb I'm going to attempt with George Bain and Dave Ganci in the middle of the Grand Canyon two months from now. But the suggestion doesn't take. A degenerative fatigue and malaise overcome me, and I repeatedly fall like a drunken sailor as I continue staggering toward Bassett Peak.

When I reach what looks like a dull mirage of that peak, dots are swirling in front of my eyes and I feel like heaving. I stick my fingers in my mouth and try to throw up in hopes of ridding myself of the debilitating bug that's apparently infected me. But I only gag and spit out a vile, bitter-tasting phlegm. I want to turn back, but there is no place to turn back to. I want there to be an easy way out of here, but I can't fly as the redtail hawks now do, soaring lazily overhead. I no longer *want* the "running power," I *need* it! But Apaches didn't come by that knowledge easily, and for a non-Indian, I now realize, it's out of my reach. I want to cry.

And I wonder if mountain man James Ohio Pattie cried when he descended from the crest of the Galiuro Mountains somewhere near here while traversing the range between March 31 and April 2, 1824. Wrote Pattie: "On the 31st, we reached the top of the mountain, and fed upon the last meat of our beavers. We met with no traces of game. . . . On the morning of the first of April, we commenced descending the mountain, from the side of which we could discern a plain before us, which, however, it required two severe days to reach . . . we had nothing to eat or drink. In descending from the icy mountains, we were surprised to find how warm it was on the plains. On reaching them, I killed an antelope, of which we drank the warm blood; and however revolting the recital may be, to us it was refreshing, tasting like fresh milk."

There are no antelope in sight to quench my thirst, even if I'd carried a gun to kill one for survival rations. I'd given up hunting and guns not long after my Grandpa Schwan died, and since then I'd resolved only to carry a knife while traveling alone in the wilderness. I am low on food, but I am too sick to hold anything down anyway. My bota bags are both dry, and my lips are cracked and bleeding. I keep running, through dirt, ice, and snow; my lungs heave in and out: *hih-huh, hih-huh, hih-huh, hih-huh*. A whirling blur of synaptic images shrouds me for hours on end in deep snow and vicious brush. Tiny acacia thorns tear at me like the claws of a thousand scrawny alley cats, and they always win, shredding my arms and legs with painfully long, blood-streaked scratches. My movement is more atavistic than conscious. I'm getting colder. I keep running. I've got to find the sign. I'm now drooling.

By the time I reach the weather-blasted trail marker sticking out of the brush like a sawed-off street sign, I'm reduced to a whimpering little boy who strayed too far from home. What looks like huge block letters proves that, despite the fear and doubt I had traveling blindly through the brush, my dead reckoning was right: RATTLESNAKE CREEK. There it is! It's my ticket back from oblivion.

I think.

And I start mumbling with joy as I gallop off the west side of an unnamed peak called BM 7,099 confident that I know the way back home. I am nothing more than a runner now; I no longer have a personal identity as I once knew it. I am merely movement from one physical clue to the next. And each time I sniff out a blaze mark on a tree, an old piece of trail, a small pile of rocks, I cry out, relieved that I'm actually tying this incipient track together through the feline jungle of upper Rattlesnake Creek.

I follow the serpentine path back and forth into the underbrush until it deadends in the catclaw. WHEOOWW!!! I backtrack, always running, but they're all deadends now. I throw up, but I am too cold and anxious to stop and clean the foul slime off my shirt. So down I go, hopping from one boulder to the next, moving not as the runner I once knew, but more like an infantile animal trying to make sense of the tenuous footing along the sharp rocks and narrow walls of the creek. This is treacherous ground, even if I wasn't sick. One slip and it'll be a bloody and agonizing crawl out of here to God knows where. I can't think about the consequences, though, or the mere thought of breaking a leg or of reinjuring my stiff ankle will distract me long enough to turn my sublimated fears into reality. All I can do now is move, instinctively. Running.

Gravity and declivity control my running speed, until I am going faster and faster; the painful jarring shudders through my legs as if somebody is whipping them against the ground. WHAP! WHAP! WHAP! But I can't stop. A furious series of steep drops unreels before me and I continue leaping like a wild man until I suddenly realize I'm making seven-foot jumps back and forth across a creek, and it's running with water. I stop, frequently, and gulp the untreated water from my cupped hands, but never for more than a few moments at a time. Running is everything now.

The setting sun is blanketing Rattlesnake Canyon with a cold shadow just as I reach the old Power's Mine road, and my running becomes a race with the edge of that shadow wall. If I can somehow stay ahead of it before it reaches Power's Garden, everything will be all right, but if that dark veil eclipses my arrival, well, I'm scared. It's not even a thought process, only a reaction to the tenuous threshold between day and night.

It's twilight when I finally reach Power's Garden, which I'd been promising myself was the end of this run. "Chris!" I scream. No answer. "Chris! . . . Chris!" Still no answer. Frenzied, I start racing around the old line shack, but it's bolted shut. Signs warn to stay the hell out. I try to busy my mind with synaptic images of this historic homestead. 1918, a tragic shootout, the largest manhunt in the history of Arizona . . . but I can't take my mind off Chris; I imagine the worst. Where is she?

I'd first met Chris in the Valley of the Sun a year earlier. Her reputation as a photographer preceded her, and we frequently talked by phone. Our friendship grew and we decided to join forces, move back to Prescott, and split living expenses.

The cheapest, most respectable place we could find was a small studio apartment next to a funeral home. We pow-wowed over the workspace, and it was agreed that I could use the kitchen table throughout the summer to bang out my novel of love, violence, and native pathways called *White Coyote . . . Running,* while Chris remodeled the small bathroom into a darkroom where she turned out masterful prints.

Frequent visits to Chris's darkroom revealed the depth of her ability to capture the essence of people in her portraits. Hanging, dripping wet, from a spiderweb of thin steel wires were black-and-white images of people from a world I hadn't known before: an eight-year-old girl carrying her month-old sister through the streets of Antigua, Guatemala; a Mao tribeswoman trading opium on the Burmese border of northern Thailand; El Zarco, a Chicano sculptor, firing a Zuñiga-influenced bronze in Tepoztlán, Mexico. These were the exotic locales Chris had ventured to, and from those travels she brought back soul-stirring images that demonstrated her willingness to expose a part of herself in order to make a picture that needed no explanation. My own photographic efforts seemed like footnotes by comparison. Little did I know at the time that my intense exposure to Chris's work would leave a lasting imprint on me that would soon change the course of my own future, from that of a camera-starved actor laboring on the novel he only dreamed of starring in, to an aspiring photojournalist who, like Chris, wanted to capture the people, places, and events that shape our lives and the world in which we live.

Chris also had studied a difficult form of Buddhist meditation called *vipassana,* or "mindfulness," while in Changmai, Thailand, a few years earlier; part of the practice required Chris to walk for hours on end across a teakwood floor of a small, empty room called a *gutee,* meditating solely about the acts of walking and breathing and their individual components. So I assumed Chris was far more adept at living and working within the constraints of a suffocatingly small studio apartment while I grew restless with the prolonged inactivity writing demanded. In fact, the more I worked alongside Chris the more I came to realize that the dog work of writing bore a strong resemblance to the long, punishing sessions of homework I sometimes faced at detention after school. Photography took you outside that stultifying room to discover places and people, to see the world and life. Comparing the two, I knew a change was in the air for me.

But before I made the leap from writing to photography, I frequently broke out of my cell and roamed the mountains of Prescott looking for new and exciting places to run the daily ten miles I tried to maintain. That was the magic number, ten. I don't know where it came from, but Randy and I decided one night while running on the Salt River Indian Reservation that if you could run ten miles a day there wasn't anything you couldn't do. But running ten miles a day in the high mountains of Prescott was a whole different ball game, and that made for daily running adventures that ultimately led to my attempting Granite Mountain at about the time I burned my first shoeboxful of rejection slips.

Once I survived that wild twelve-mile run, as clumsy

and as ignorant as I'd been, I quickly embarked on a string of other runs in hopes of building on the knowledge of running wild I was learning, both through the trial and error of running through a barrage of canyons, mountains, and desert, and through ethnographic accounts and bits and pieces of historical fact I'd ferreted out during painstaking, often fruitless, hours of research at local libraries. One gem I'd discovered was about the Apaches, who used a "running power" . . .

But that's why I was now in way over my head.

I break down again and again as I run and stumble along the boulder-strewn canyon bottom, but I'm too exhausted and dehydrated to cry. Tears no longer form, and my legs are too painful to move by conscious thought; they are controlled by something beyond me now. That something is fear. Darkness completely engulfs me as I continue thrashing down the floodswept black gash of Rattlesnake Canyon, and I'm frightened beyond anything I've ever imagined.

The sound of rushing water screams at me. Tree limbs hit me like night sticks. Brush tears at me. Logs trip me. Rocks stop me, just long enough to let me know that something other than conscious thought is controlling my movement, as if I'm now outside myself watching someone else struggle through the oil-black, thigh-deep torrent. I feel weird and unworldly, as if I haven't been here before; but I *have* been here before, with Jack Cartier! The water's cold, I know it is, but it doesn't feel that way, only wet. The only thought I have now is that somehow my eyes are still open and that my body—not me—is still running. And it won't, can't stop!

The wind is gusting across Power's Hill, and I am shivering violently with cold, wet chills when I finally crawl out of Rattlesnake Canyon and head across the black plain to Aravaipa Creek. I have to stop and start a fire, now, or I'm going to die. I hastily gather black shapes of wood, but my hands tremble as my stiff fingers strip damp bark away from the dry tinder beneath; without it, there will be no fire tonight. I pile it, shaking like a madman, the tufts of tinder, the incrementally larger pieces of kindling, into a small tepee sheltered from the wind by my body, which has grown rigid with cramps; squatting there, I'm becoming a cold, knotted ball of blood, muscle, and bone. I struggle desperately to stay coherent long enough to ignite the fire.

One strike. Another. Nothing. The wind is howling around me and my body continues to shake uncontrollably. I take in a full deep breath, then exhale in an attempt to control my spastic shivering; it doesn't help. I strike the knife along the flint again. Nothing. I strike it again and again, scraping the razor-sharp steel down the length of the flint, showering the ground with a celebration of dying sparks. Nothing. I try again and again. Finally a single spark takes hold of the dry yucca fiber, and still shaking in fits and stammers, I add small bits of kindling to that tiny, miraculous flame, afraid I'll snuff it out by adding too much fuel too quickly. Piece by piece, I slowly pile on more and more wood, as if I'm stoking a furnace, until the eruption of flames singes my face and eyebrows and my body slowly begins to warm. When it does, I know I'm going to survive, and that Chris, mindfully pacing somewhere out there in the middle of the night next to her car, has been unable to ford Aravaipa Creek, which is swollen with the same runoff that boiled down Rattlesnake Canyon. Dreaming the fire, I no longer have any idea what "running power" is.

CHAPTER THREE

The Midnight Crack

> *We are the first and doubtless*
> *will be the last party of whites to*
> *visit this profitless locality.*
>
> Lt. Joseph C. Ives, April 3, 1858,
> upon entering the Grand Canyon

It is May. The hour is late. Snow has begun to fall. And the wind will not let up. We have come prepared for heat, the kind of skull-numbing heat that sweeps over the inner Canyon this time of year like a festering mirage, not the last vestiges of a brutal winter still frothing down off the North Rim.

Standing there shivering on a small ledge, four thousand three hundred and seventy odd feet above the roaring Colorado River, we have to make a decision—I have to make a decision. Should we continue climbing for the summit in the hopes of finding enough firewood to survive a bivouac at 7,123 feet? Or do we attempt a long and dangerous retreat down the southwest face of Zoroaster Temple in the dead of night? That's where the three of us are perched now, on a monolithic sandstone temple in the middle of the Grand Canyon, and we're burning daylight. Worse, we are anchored to a spaghettilike confusion of nylon rope; our teeth are clattering from the cold, and we

49

are hopping in place like old men waiting for the light to change on a blustery winter evening.

I look at my partners.

Dave Ganci, the bearded "pioneer" among us, had been here two decades earlier; that's when he and climbing partner Rick Tidrick pulled off the audacious first ascent of Zoroaster Temple, when other climbers were only dreaming about it. In doing so, Dave and Tidrick not only climbed the most magnificent temple in the Grand Canyon, they also proved rock climbing techniques first pioneered in Yosemite Valley could be used to climb what were once thought to be the Canyon's unscalable "summits below the rim." So a first ascent of the southwest face wasn't as important to Dave as it was to me. Besides, his stomach still felt as if someone had buried his fist in it and left it there.

George Bain, on the other hand, is a Colorado River boatman and a veteran Grand Canyon climber with an impressive list of Canyon ascents to his credit, including a new route up Zoroaster's north side the year before; if push came to shove, George could live with that for another year or so.

Me, I've never climbed on anything remotely as mesmerizing as Zoroaster before, except in my mind over a brew with these two lads. But having been touched by Zoroaster's magic, I am now so drawn to its summit that little else seems to matter—except the safety of my partners. That's why I'm frantically trying to sort out the pros and cons as objectively as possible, given the fact that I personally have a lot riding on Zoroaster. It's the first difficult new route I've attempted since my fall; I knew going in that if my ankle could withstand the rigors of the long approach to Zoroaster's base, I could at least entertain the possibilities of embarking on a career of Himalayan climbing. But if my ankle fell apart en route to Zoroaster, I always had running, running wild, I'd thought. But shortly after crawling out of

Rattlesnake Canyon two months earlier, I even had grave doubts about that and about whether I'd be able to take running wild to the limits I'd first imagined. Tossing and turning around the dying embers of the lonely bivouac fire back then, my left ankle had been seized with such pain that I thought I was back on Squaw Peak; because, come daybreak, I had been forced to use an agave stalk to crutch and hobble another dozen miles out to my rendezvous with Chris on Aravaipa Creek. The Galiuros had driven me toward a troubling crossroads in my life, and by climbing the southwest face I hoped to be able to choose the path I was truly destined for: climbing or running—I couldn't master both.

Still, if I decide to push on, the three of us will be drawn into yet another dangerous race, a race with darkness. We've already lost our first race, the one with water. Natural springs and perennial streams are as few in the Grand Canyon as they are difficult to reach, and so most of the water we needed for the climb had to be carried: a gallon a day per head, eight and a half pounds a gallon. Combined with enough climbing gear, ropes, and food to attempt a first ascent of what already had repulsed several other strong parties, the weight and unwieldiness of the water sloshing around inside our monstrous packs made our knees buckle—and my ankle scream. Even so, we knew three gallons each wouldn't be enough water to reach Zoroaster, do the climb, and drop all the way back down to Phantom Ranch at the river. So once we had established our base camp at the foot of Zoroaster, we replenished our dwindling supply with water George had cached the year before and with a *tinaja* Dave and I had found at the foot of neighboring Brahma Temple. But when Dave put his lips to that shallow catchment of rain water, he sucked out a nasty intestinal amoeba called giardia, and it tracked him like a marked man throughout the day.

Then, we've been on Zoroaster since sunup, slowly and

methodically free-climbing our way up five rope-lengths of fossilized sand, which, at high noon, absorbed the warm rays of the sun like a vertical beach. We stripped down accordingly and savored each airy pitch, because we were climbing in a natural arena which, seen as a great inverted mountain range, literally sucked the wind out of you with its scale; that and the fact we were on an isolated pinnacle of rock surrounded on all sides by thousands of feet of heart-stopping exposure. But none of us has had any water since noon, and that had been only a few mouthfuls each. It is now 5:28 P.M., and the severe fluid deficit I figure each of us is working on is beginning to exact a toll.

But the dark pall of night, that is my biggest fear now; never mind the threat that these wild, wind-whipped snow flurries might turn into a savage snowstorm that could bury us on our perch. If night lies down on us before we reach the Toroweap summit blocks, neither George nor I will be any more fit to lead than Dave now is. I'm not sure about George, but up until now night climbing has not been my specialty.

George and Dave continue to look at me; their eyes tell me they can go either way. Just make the decision. Seconds continue to tick by, but I am stymied because I'm held rapt by the scene before us. Staring back across the Canyon like an awestruck tourist, I can see, through the swirling snow, the faint outline of the seven-thousand foot high Coconino Plateau; it tumbles off its southern escarpment from one horizon to the next like a great tidal wave of rock collapsing en masse atop the thin, turbulent strand of the Colorado River a vertical mile below. As heavily laden as we'd been during the approach, it had taken us a full day to reach the river from the South Rim through that brink, even though the declivitous South Kaibab Trail provided the quickest route through the clifflike layers of neapolitan rock that might otherwise have proved insurmountable. But once we headed north from the river, we had had to rely on Dave's and George's recall of a largely trailless route that ascended the slick black Vishnu schist, the terrifyingly rotten Redwall band, and the bloodstained Hermit shale; in the process we had climbed back up almost another vertical mile to reach the foot of this huge, flat-topped horn of Coconino sandstone that squatted atop its Supai sandstone foundation as if it had been mushed down on a base of burnt orange wax. Yet Zoroaster was not alone; because before us and all around us stood other spires and buttes, which, like Zoroaster, also resembled the dwelling places of deities. Then, that was part of the fascination and irresistable lure of climbing in the Grand Canyon, the fact that many of the Canyon's isolated temples had been named by geologist and cartographer Clarence Dutton after the temples he'd visited in the Orient during the 1800s; they were too sublime to be named after mere mortals, Dutton had thought. Better to call them names like Tower of Ra, Confucius, Angel's Gate, Buddha. . .

"Annerino! What do you want to do?"

Jerked from my twilight revery by the harsh reality of the moment, I turn back and ask George, "Got any matches?" I knew the answer even before I asked it. I just wanted some reassurance that, if we actually succeeded in climbing to the summit in the dark, we would at least be able to build a bivouac fire.

"Yeah," George says. The word hangs there momentarily, before it is swept away by a chill wind into the depths of the Canyon.

That is that; I have no excuses. "All right, I'll make you a deal," I say.

"What's that?" George yells above the wind, mindful of the fact that I once worked on a car lot.

"You lead that," I say, pointing to the horrendous pitch looming above, "and I'll lead that."

His orange parka flapping crazily in the wind, George

looks up and sees the two casket-sized blocks we'd seen earlier; it doesn't look like it will take much to dislodge them and to squash, like melons, anybody in their deadly fall line. Faced with that prospect, I have no illusions about trying to make the nerve-jangling moves around them myself. George isn't exactly enchanted with the prospect, either, because if he blows a move on this pitch, it most likely will end in a flesh-ripping, bone-crushing pendulum against the opposite wall. A long fall down a smooth face or into an overhang was an acceptable risk for me, but the pain still throbbing in my ankle forcefully reminded me to avoid those leads that involved ledges—or abrupt stops of any kind.

Apparently having worked out the moves in his head, George peers beyond his lead into mine. "You want it bad enough to lead that, in the dark?" he asks.

"I'd rather climb at night than rappel at night," I tell him. But as soon as I say that I realize there really isn't any other choice; if we're to survive the night and get off this thing alive, we have to climb. Our hand has been forced. Unlike climbing, which melds mind and body to rock, rappelling requires a climber to rely almost completely on the mechanics of anchors and rigging. The history of climbing is tragically littered with the bodies of world-class climbers who, at one distracted moment, died because they clipped or unclipped the wrong carabiner.

"You lead the traverse, George, and I'll do the rest," I say.

Each of us, I realize, holds the key for the others; without them both, the door to the summit will remain locked, and the three of us will be forced to rappel one nauseating rope-length after another into the dark and who knows what kind of fatal mistakes awaiting below. Clad only in flimsy parkas and heavy sweaters, we are too cold to remain at an impasse. Buffeted by strong, fickle gusts of wind,

George starts up. Snow pelts his red beard, and his gold earring swings back and forth like a noiseless wind chime.

"You got me, Annerino?"

A nerve-rattling half-hour later George is on the crux. If he makes the moves, we will at least be guaranteed a stance at the bottom of the final pitch; if not, he will take a sixty-foot fall, pendulum like a yo-yo slammed against a curb, and probably unhinge those two huge blocks on top of us.

"I got you!" I yell.

I am scared. Dave gives me one of his oh-shit-this-is-it looks. We both remember the twenty-five-foot fall George took earlier in the day; it jerked me up in the air so violently that it felt as if I'd been pulled off the ledge by a rescue helicopter's skyhook; in the process, the three bushes Dave and I were "anchored" to had been practically uprooted. It was a thin line, to be sure, and who knew how many fragile roots had prevented the three of us, all roped together like a bolo, from hurtling over the yawning drop of Zoroaster Amphitheater to our water cache three thousand feet below. A masonry bolt would have precluded that horrible possibility, but we were trying to climb "clean."

In the failing light I make out the dark figure of George as he reaches across the crux through the falling snow. It is a desperately awkward move. The key handhold is just beyond his reach, an inch maybe, no more than two. He pauses for a moment; when he does, I know he is steeling himself before he tries to put the moves together. There won't be a second chance. At that instant, I try to detach myself from the reality of the moment; if he falls, I know what it means and there's nothing I can do about it. Dave also seems resigned to the moment. As for George, I can feel the tension of his right leg resonate down the length of rope into my cold hands.

George has to do it now; we all know it.

As if prompted by some atavistic memory, George stretches back down even farther than he had before. He paws the hold, gingerly at first to make sure it won't slough off in his fingers, and when he knows the hold is sound, I can feel the relief reverberate back down the length of rope. George steps across and screams. He's done it! That small hold was the key to the Twilight Traverse, and George was the only one among us who could have made the moves to climb past it.

"Guess it's my turn," I say to Dave. He nods silently, still holding his stomach.

George ties off and puts me on belay. I start climbing up his perilous vertical puzzle, confident that I am now safeguarded by a taut rope protecting me from above. With night almost upon us, there is no time to remove the anchors George had so carefully placed during his difficult lead. I climb past each dangling nut. Once I stretch around the two huge blocks, I grasp what remains of the gear rack from George and sling it nooselike around my neck and shoulders.

"Your turn," George says, puffing on a leftover piece of stogie. The brightness of the burning ember is a gauge against which to measure the depth of the darkness and the cold that now dictates our movements.

"Glad I didn't lead that!" I tell George, half hoping he'll be swept up by the camaraderie of the moment and volunteer to lead my pitch as well. But George has earned his stogie-lit perch; alone, I have to earn mine high above.

"Wait till you see the off-width," he says, trying to laugh off the last of his fears.

"I don't want to look at it, George." He laughs again, and we wait, carefully nursing the bitter-tasting cigar stump between us, occasionally refiring it with George's snow- and windproof lighter.

It's around midnight when Dave finally reaches us. The wind is still blowing, dusting our eyelashes and thighs with dry spindrift, a promising sign that we may have escaped a full-scale storm. Dave ties off next to George. As long as it's taken him to jumar and clean the pitch, I assume he's really sick; I don't even broach the subject of his leading the last pitch.

I grab the flashlight out of his mouth and stick the gnawed-on, wet plastic handle in mine. It is my lead, Dave's belay. There is no time for backslapping. Darkness has already beaten us at its game, and we are losing a grim third race with cold and fatigue. George has since climbed lizardlike out of the blowing snow and in between two boulders. He knows, as we all do, that I won't exactly sprint up the Midnight Crack.

Tentatively, I start up. The small Duracell-powered beam shines the way, but I don't need the light to know I am groping through a layer of mud that forms the mortar between the Coconino sandstone and Toroweap limestone; it is too soft and crumbly to permit a solid purchase with either my slick-soled boots or my fingertips. The hard metal climbing tools and crampons of an iceman would have been more suitable for this appalling layer, but who could have guessed that while viewing the southwest face from the South Rim four days earlier? I hadn't. So I take the climbing a foot at a time, aware that Dave may be dozing off, unable to stave off the irresistible pull of sleep.

Carefully removing my right hand from a crumbly hold, I take the light out of my mouth and shout into the blackness below.

"Dave! . . . Hey Dave! . . . You awake?" I can't do this alone.

" . . . huh . . . yeah, I gotcha!"

I tug at the rope and continue groping, as if I'm trying to find my way up out of a dark, muddy cavern. Fatigue is wrapping its deadly arms around me, and it feels as if I'm about to be yanked into the abyss. I want desperately to sleep. Cold is slashing at me like a hundred painful cuts from a razor. I don't want to be alone, but I feel as if I'm on the edge of the earth and about to tumble off into an endless free-fall. Somehow, I have to stay awake—just long enough to finish the lead. I mouth my upper lip between my eye-teeth and the plastic flashlight casing; whenever fatigue darts in I bite down until I can feel the pain, the warm trickle of blood. I am climbing for my life.

With each grungy foot I gain, I yell back down to Dave, flashlight in mouth: "Dave! . . . Hey Dave, you awake?"

But it always takes a second or third cry from me to pry a response out of him: " . . . yeah . . . yeah, I gotcha'."

I'm not sure how much rope I've run out, but once I climb over the crumbly edge of mud I arrive at the base of a chimney and decide to place a bolt; under normal conditions it wouldn't be necessary, but fear has stampeded over me. Worse, I am high above my sleeping belayer with no anchors between us, except for two questionable nuts maybe thirty feet below; even when I placed them I realized they were only psychological protection, just enough to trick myself into climbing the next five or ten feet to "easier" ground. That is the ruse, and I've used it to reach the foot of the Midnight Crack.

I fumble for the bolt driver and commence hammering, occasionally hitting my left hand instead of my intended mark, but it is too cold to feel the full force of the steel hammerhead as it slams against my bare knuckles. The bolt placed, I clip into it and fight my way into the base of the chimney. I'm safe in here, I think to myself once inside; there's no exposure. There's no exposure at night, anyway, so what am I thinking? I am getting groggier; I bite down harder, and start climbing again. With my knees and palms pressed against the wall in front of me, and with my heels, buttocks, and shoulders counterpressured wedgelike behind me, I shinny up. Wriggling awkwardly, I feel as if I'm going to be spit out of the crack at any moment, because for every foot I gain I slip half a foot back.

Temporarily wedged, I shine the light high above to expose a series of sinister-looking chockstones; they look like bombs about to drop on me. As I struggle through this bomb bay, I carefully thread each of them with nylon webbing and clip my rope to them, wondering how short a fall it would take to avalanche the lot of them. Swearing, grunting, still biting my lip, I know that if I slip I won't fall far within this chimney; the chockstones will wedge my broken legs and back solidly against the twin walls of this vertical tomb.

If I am lucky, the chimney will continue to widen above and end in a secure, womblike cave leading to the summit. I follow it, hoping this subterranean fantasy will come true. But the higher I climb, the more disoriented I become. It's so dark that I have no real sense of up or down; I know only that *this* is the way I entered the chimney, so *that's* the way I continue to travel—head first, until I smash my helmet on the ceiling above. When I do, my worst fears are confirmed: dead end. Fear and loathing race me back down thirty feet of the most desperate climbing I've ever done. As long as I control my breathing, I don't have to down-climb; my body, pulsating like a giant slug sliding down a crack in the sidewalk, prevents me from falling.

I can see nothing below me except Arizona's version of the Black Hole; there is precious little above me and all around me, except night. If I'm about to die, I want to do it in control, climbing as I never have before. Above me, I know, is the off-width George and I had seen from below. It is the crux of the Midnight Crack, and it defies me to enter it.

Firmly believing I'm about to die, I thread the last chockstone with a nylon runner, insert my left hand and

arm in the overhanging fissure above, and squeeze and con-
tort my limb until it feels like a ten-penny nail has been
driven into my shoulder. I try to focus all my energy in my
pain-wracked left arm, and when I pull down on it with all
my might, it feels as if I'm going to pull all of Zoroaster
down on top of me. When I realize the temple is not going
to topple, I stem my right leg against the wall in front of me,
but I repeatedly miss the crucial nubbin with my quivering
right foot. I begin shaking all over. My left arm feels like it's
starting to dislocate, and I feel myself start to go. I scream,
and begin sobbing until the cries stop as quickly as they'd
started.

"I gotcha, John!"

"Get us off here, Annerino!"

But their voices are from another world, both of them
straining to see that which they cannot: a fading pinprick of
light crawling toward the dark heavens.

I never could do a one-arm pullup, so I take in a deep
breath and grab my left forearm with my free hand to pre-
vent my shoulder from tearing out of its socket. Hanging
there by my fist, I relax my right leg as best I can, then point
the toe of my boot at a small nubbin of rock, now show-
cased by a narrow, flickering beam of light. The batteries
are starting to go and I can taste the salt trickling out the
side of my mouth. My arched leg quivers like a wand bend-
ing in a breeze, but my boot kisses the nubbin. Once, twice,
I can feel it by touch, and when the light comes back on I
can actually see it again. I press against the nubbin, caressing
it at first to make sure it's not going to flake off; slowly, it
takes the pressure of my weight, I stand up on it and the immense burden is lifted from my twisted, pain-wracked arm.

Relief surges over me like a warm, gentle wave when I
realize I'm negotiating the crux; but I beat back this small
feeling of pleasure before it overcomes me and strands me
thirty feet below the summit. It's happened to better

climbers, so there's no reason it can't happen to me. With both arms I dig furiously into the crack above. I brace my bruised left knee below, push off with my right leg, and move up again. Just a few more feet and it's over . . .

When I crawl over the edge of summit block I spit the flashlight out of my mouth and collapse. I fall into a fitful, almost fatal doze. I don't think about it; it's just that death seems so passive in the cold and I welcome the rest, at long last.

Someone's calling me, but I must be dreaming; I blink my eyes and I still can't see anything. It's suddenly bitterly cold, and stereo voices are screaming:

"Annerino . . . Hey, Annerino! You awake?"

I draw my left leg up—it has been dangling over the edge—and crawl mindlessly on my hands and knees to the nearest bush, where I "anchor" the rope. I remember wiping blood off the side of my mouth before yelling into the center of the earth: "All right, we're up!"

II

We are lost in the steel-gray mist of first light, three small figures huddled next to the damp, smoldering coals of a dying fire. We are anxious. At any moment the sun is going to erupt out of the Desert Facade far to the east . . . when it does, it shrouds us in an ethereal orange mist that stirs the drifting smoke of our fire as if we've been seated around a magic lantern all night. We are groggy and our bodies feel cold and burnt—burned on the front side from restoking the fire through the waning hours of night, bone chilled on the backside from the force of the wind. We are stiff, sore, hungry, and thirsty. And my ankle feels as if a wolf's been gnawing on it all night in hopes of crunching through the leg bone for the sweet marrow within. But we are alive atop majestic Zoroaster Temple, and we are suddenly enveloped by the spherical prism of the rising sun, and it feels like we're being projected through a holograph where time, distance and pain are temporarily suspended.

Levitating in the middle of this Canyon sea until its fleeting visual magic dissipates, the sun slowly bakes the deep chill out of our haggard bodies, and I drift back into the last burning embers of our fire while Dave and George rustle from their own half-sleep. I've been dreaming the fire off and on throughout the night, and in its burning-red core I've seen a recurring image: a man, running alone, half-naked through the Grand Canyon. I'm not sure who it was; it was just a figure running through the dancing red-and-orange flames as my head drooped on and off my chest. But he—it—was running east to west through the Canyon as far as I can now see; through the clouds that part as if a curtain has been rolled back to reveal a colossal amphitheater. From the mouth of the Little Colorado River Gorge, where it spills its cerulean blue waters into the muddy Colorado River, the tiny figure ran west along the broad, undulating platform of the Tonto formation, one-hundred-fifty stories above the turgid river . . . and he didn't stop until he reached the tier of turquoise water falls spewing out of Havasupai at the other end of the Canyon.

That's all it was, an image of a man running through a Canyon dreamscape, anyman, everyman, and it stays with me as the three of us rope off the backside of Zoroaster like three thieves who have just pulled off the heist of their lives. But as soon as I shoulder my heavy pack at the foot of Zoroaster, I know who that figure is, because my ankle starts screaming at me like an old fishwife. It's an argument I've lost before, and this time it lasts the two days it takes us to stagger back out to the South Rim under heavy loads. En route, however, I'm too leery to mention my dream to Dave or George, or even to Chris, who'd kept the vigil of a one-woman support crew and expedition photographer at our basecamp throughout the night. The idea is too preposterous: running end to end through someplace I am having a difficult enough time just trying to crawl out of?

I wait until I return to Prescott, where I am soothed by the warm winds of summer blowing through the pines outside my Groom Creek cabin, before I phone Tim Ganey. He will tell me if I've gone off the deep end, or if there is the remotest possibility that somebody, anybody, could run the length of the Grand Canyon.

I first met Tim in high school when a beautiful lass named Kathleen Jowdy hog-tied both our hearts. Kathleen had long, brown hair she sometimes festooned with ribbons at the ends of her wavy locks, a warm smile that made your knees weak, and class that overshadowed her peers. But Tim had the schoolboy charm and Redford good looks, and he won Kathleen's heart hands down. Instead of butting heads over Kathleen or even drifting apart, though, Tim and I grew closer, drawn together by the same unending flow of adolescent dreams and ideas. But there was another force at work between Tim and me, too; more often than not, each of us already knew what the other was thinking without having mentioned it. And I came to trust Tim's perspective and judgment implicitly. If anybody could realistically grasp the concept of a man running through the Grand Canyon, Tim could. I ring him up.

"What do you think, honestly, Tim?"

"I think it's a great idea."

"But nobody's ever done it before," I protest.

"John"—Tim always used your first name like an exclamation point if he wanted your undivided attention—"that's exactly why we should do it."

Tim's enthusiasm is contagious, and it infects Craig Hudson, a close friend of his. So the three of us rendezvous at my cabin to sort the whole thing out. Is it really possible to do what no one else has even attempted, or is this one of those Mike Johnson ideas that comes from so far out in left field you can't believe it unless you do it yourself? And, if it is possible, can we, like Johnson, actually deliver? We try to answer those basic questions when we roll the topographical map of Grand Canyon National Park across the pine-dusted wooden floor of my front porch; when we do, it is as if we've suddenly pried open a dark, jagged crack in the earth that exposes all my deepest fears. Sitting there, we wonder what would happen if we view the Brobdingnagian fissure we are staring into as a Himalayan mountain turned inside out. Can we, having sustained ourselves, in part, on a diet of Chris Bonnington adventures, apply the same mountaineering principles to running end to end through the Canyon? Viewing the Canyon from that perspective, we think we see a way to resupply a runner with the same kinds of tactics Bonnington used to tackle Himalayan giants like the south face of Annapurna and the southwest face of Everest. But instead of using a base camp and advance base camp at the foot of a mountain to support a continuous string of camps leading to a summit, we can establish a roving base camp atop the South Rim, which will send support-crew members into the inner Canyon to establish one-night camps as the runner journeys east to west through the heart of the Grand Canyon.

In theory, it seems a sound approach. And instead of our meeting falling apart under the preposterousness of the idea, Tim and Craig suddenly see a way to reach out for what I now believe is beyond my own grasp. When they do, they grow serious; if I am ready to commit to it, they will do whatever it takes to get me through the Grand Canyon; all they want out of it is to be part of a team that can pull off the seemingly impossible.

Coming on the heels of Zoroaster—I dragged my left foot all the way back out to the South Rim like an old suitcase—it doesn't take me long to commit to running the Grand Canyon. My ankle, I am beginning to realize, might never recover sufficiently to climb an eight thousand–meter peak. I know I could endure the pain of the two-week approach marches required to reach most Himalayan base camps, but what would happen, I wonder, if my ankle suddenly knotted up with pain when I was, say, on an icy ridge high atop Dhaulagiri, or on the south col of Everest? What kind of irreversible plank would I be walking? Worse, what kind of potentially tragic scenario would that paint my teammates into? Seen in that light, running the Grand Canyon suddenly becomes the shining path in my life; I can attempt to run through a canyon that was on the scale of a Himalayan peak, and that will challenge me with the same kinds of objective dangers, but if my ankle blows apart en route I'll be the only one running the red line, because I'll be running it solo. And because I really have no way to gauge the scale of my undertaking, I have every reason to believe there is a strong possibility I might die trying, so I train with the knowledge that I am about to face the Goliath of canyons. So I pound out a daily training regimen to supplement my running, slowly increasing my daily running mileage so that by the time I leave for the Canyon I'll be able confidently to run half the mileage I will need to average between waterholes each day. And on weekends I run a seemingly endless treadmill of canyons, mesas, deserts, and mountains in hopes of simulating every kind of environmental condition and physical obstacle I will encounter in the Canyon. I also want to steel myself for the psychological uncertainty and loneliness of running terrain I've never explored before.

Fortunately, most of these wilderness runs don't turn into the life-and-death struggle the Galiuros had; in running those mountains end to end, I realize I've made too big a leap too quickly. So I increase the length of these long runs incrementally until I can run 25 to 35 miles without caving in to fatigue. Still, one run stands out among all the others in a way that makes me reexamine my motives for running wild in general, and for running the Grand Canyon in particular.

It was a sunny day in February, and I was running alone through the wind-brushed desert of Organ Pipe Cactus National Monument toward old Mexico. Dave was tailing me somewhere in the distance. Pushed by a strong tailwind, I was streaking across a *bajada* that fanned out from the base of the Bates Mountains when I suddenly noticed two sets of bare footprints; they were coming from the south and were headed northeast across the thorny desert. Barefoot! Now, I knew I was following an old smugglers' route that led out of Sonora to Phoenix via the desolate back roads of the Tohono O'odham (formerly Papago) lands, but what I didn't discover until some time later was that the tracks I followed south another fifteen miles to the ancient Sand Papago encampment of Quitobaquito Springs on the U.S.–Mexico border were those of Mexican citizens. They were headed north 50 to 120 grueling miles across the most deadly desert in North America in the hopes of finding work in the U.S. Most often, they attempted those desperately heroic treks in the summer, when conditions could not possibly be worse but when farm labor jobs were most plentiful. Needless to say, not all of them made it; in fact, estimates at the time ran to hundreds who perished while "commuting to work."

But this was also the same merciless desert the Tohono O'odham crossed, sometimes running, when they embarked on their own grueling midsummer journeys to gather salt on the shores of the Sea of Cortez, when they sang during this ritual spirit quest:

Then in the west a wind arose,
Well knowing whither it should blow.
Up rose a mist and towered toward the sky,
And others stood with it, their tendrils touching.
Then they moved.
Although the earth seemed very wide,
Clear to the edge of it did they go.

And this was the same fearsome *despoblado* (uninhabited land) that *El Camino del Diablo*, the Highway of the Devil, traversed en route to the promised land that the Spaniards called Alta California. From the time Padre Eusebio Kino first crossed these sun-scorched ancestral lands of the ancient *Areneños*, or Sand Papago, in 1699, El Camino claimed hundreds of lives; in the 1850s alone, historians believe, at least four hundred gold seekers, many of them Mexican nationals, died of thirst en route to the California goldfields. What, I wondered, did the modern "gold seekers" think about, and why were they still following an ancient path of fire that paralleled the timeless tracks of the Tohono O'odham along a route most modern athletes couldn't survive? I didn't know. But it only made me more curious about the historic routes and trails and the ancient ways of Native American running and pathways. Where did the pathways lead? Why and when were they used? And what could it have possibly been like to run them? Slowly, I began piecing shreds of answers together; and as I did, I came to realize that a maze of ancient pathways still crisscrossed the Southwest and the frontier of northern Mexico, and I began to view them as a means of retracing the roots of running back to its source.

Marathons and 10Ks held little meaning for me. What, Hunter S. Thompson asked in *The Curse of Lono*, "would cause 8,000 supposedly smart people to get up at four in the morning and stagger at high speed through the streets of

Waikiki for 26 ball-busting miles in a race that less than a dozen of them have the slightest chance of winning?" And on hard, black pavement made for automobiles, I mused, not for the rhythmic pounding of moccasined feet running to the beat of a natural lifeway that inextricably linked running with hunting and gathering, culture and travel, ritual and religion, a tribe's very identity and survival? After a while I began to see even my own wilderness running as the same uneventful motion I saw in marathons and 10Ks; there seemed little point in it, unless I could somehow rediscover something—anything—about the dawn of Native American running that would infuse my own running with substance and meaning, something that would take it into another dimension.

Retracing those bare footprints across the desert to their source was the turning point for me, and it made me view my own running and my proposed Canyon pathway in a new light. Yet as much research as I did and as hard as I was training, I was never sure it was enough. Native American runners grew up running long distances, but I was only a recent convert to it. So I ran harder and longer, until sometimes I would just "dorph out" and stare mindlessly at the food on my plate; my brain would be reeling, addled by endorphins, the body's natural opiate. When I discovered the dorph factor, I realized that no matter how stiff my ankle might be at the beginning of a run the endorphins would kick in, at some point the pain would vanish, and I would feel as though I were running on air.

Then I was running so much at seven thousand feet above sea level that I began having vivid and startling dreams about just that, running on air. The dream always started out the same. I'd be running through the fog-shrouded woods up the road from my cabin, and ever so slowly, my strides would get longer and longer, and I would stay in the air a second or two longer with each footstep, until eventually I was actually floating, running above the ground. If I'd gobbled drugs or smoked dope, I might have understood why I was having these dreams, but I didn't; water, coffee, aspirin, orange juice, and beer were my elixirs to prepare for or come down from a running high. Then, maybe the dreams had something to do with the fact that I was hypnotized by the research I was doing on the Tibetan trance runners called *lung gom-pas,* and on the "secret way of running" some Southwest Native Americans reportedly used, and maybe the imagery just carried over into my dreams. There was no explaining it. But each time I had the flying-running dream—and I had it more and more frequently as my departure date drew nearer—I could have sworn I'd actually, physically, run two to three feet above the ground.

Then, I was going to need some kind of edge if I was going to be able to follow my pathway even halfway through the Canyon. So I began visualizing the course of my pathway, day by day, until there wasn't any part of it I couldn't clearly call up to memory while running; it was the same way I'd envisioned the Galiuros as a capital H and the mental image I had of that route. Only, I didn't just visualize each section of my inner-Canyon pathway, I tried to envision myself running along a narrow, crumbly ledge high above the river through an endless V-bottomed tunnel that twisted and turned into forever, one day at a time. It was just too overwhelming for me to focus on the whole Grand Canyon and on an image of running it in one fell swoop, but by breaking it up into sections its stupendous scale became manageable—at least from a psychological standpoint.

That's the way many of the Canyon's earliest foot travelers took the Canyon, in sections. Take the prospectors who swept in a wave over the Grand Canyon in the 1870s, many of them believing they were about to unearth the mother lode somewhere in the depths of what they must certainly have envisioned as an open-air treasure chest; only, to reach their dream fields they had to chisel trails down from the North and South rims into what some tribes, among them the Hopi, revered as the very center of the earth. Many of the miners' trails either followed or paralleled those first used by the Anasazi, the "Ancient Ones"; like the Desert Culture that preceded them by thousands of years, the Anasazi trekked in and out of the Canyon on a seasonal basis, to grow food on the fertile deltas along the river's edge or to hunt deer on the forested rims high above. Archaeologists also believe the Anasazi climbed many of the Canyon's less technical temples and buttes about A.D. 1000, in order to collect flint, to hunt deer and bighorn sheep, and to gather the agave hearts they roasted in earthen hearths called yanta ovens.

But the faint trails of the Anasazi, and the eighty-four miners' trails that reportedly shadowed them at one time, plunged off the edge of the Canyon directly into its depths, in rim-to-river fashion. And while early river explorers and adventurers like James White and Major John Wesley Powell traveled the length of the Canyon by log raft and boat, there is little evidence that early man traveled end to end through the Canyon on foot. Mormon missionary and explorer Jacob Hamblin was believed to be the first white man to journey completely *around* the Grand Canyon in 1862. But even someone as experienced as Hamblin was forced to eat crow before he completed his five-hundred mile loop atop the Colorado plateau: " . . . we were very short of food . . . [and] we lay by one day on the Pahreah, and killed and cooked crows to help our rations." On the other hand, historians and anthropologists have a fair record of tribes like the Paiute *crossing* the western Grand Canyon from the North Rim to the South in order to trade and visit with the Havasupai, but the only people known to enter the Grand Canyon from the east and to travel any distance to the west were the Hopi. The Hopi periodically made sacred salt pilgrimages from their villages on First, Second, and Third mesas a hundred-odd miles west to the mouth of the Little Colorado River Gorge, an immense chasm they would follow west into the hidden recesses of the Grand Canyon and their sacred salt mines. No one knows for certain whether they ventured beyond those mines, westward along the Tonto formation. However, what *is* known is that the early Hopi were formidable runners. Perhaps the best account of this comes from the August 1909 edition of *The Border;* in an article titled "Life and Its Living in Hopiland," Kate T. Cory wrote:

> It is doubtful if any tribes of Indians or any groups of white men in the country can average with the Hopi in running: it is instinctive with him; wherever he goes afoot, if any distance, he runs, striking a rapid springy trot, the right arm crooked, and working back and forth as he speeds along; and he seems not to know what it means to tire.
>
> Thirty miles a day to Keams Canyon is an any day jaunt for him; and the railroad, sixty-five miles away, he makes if a good runner easily before sunset. The record is held by an old man, now in the happy hunting ground (the "Skeleton House" the Hopis have it), who, so the story goes, ran to Moencoppi, nearly fifty miles away, and back each day throughout the summer, spending an hour there working in his fields.

There was also an ancient rim-top trade route that linked the Hopi villages with the Havasupai two hundred miles to the west. Accounts by Spanish missionary Francisco Tomás Garcés in 1775–76 document the fact that the Hopi used this route to trade with the Havasupai, but it's not known whether they used the route regularly or during which seasons. If they traveled the route in winter, what would they do if they found it buried under several feet of snow? Wouldn't it be more logical for them to have followed the Little Colorado River Gorge westward beyond their salt mines and to continue through the balmier depths of the inner Canyon to Havasupai? The Anasazi (not to be confused with the Hopi or any other culturally and linguistically distinct tribe of prehistoric or historic Native Americans) made seasonal migrations into the depths of the Canyon, so why couldn't the Hopi also have used an inner Canyon route during the harsh winter months if they needed to trade with the Havasupai? And, if they did follow an inner Canyon trade route, wouldn't it have been far more efficient for them to have run it? There are historic and modern eyewitness accounts of Chihuahua's Tarahumara running, for days on end, several hundred miles through Mexico's *Barranca del Cobre,* a canyon region, reportedly larger than the mile-deep, two thousand square-mile region formed by the Grand Canyon; to me, that analogy constituted irrefutable proof that it was at least feasible for Native Americans to have run through the Grand Canyon.

The Tarahumara had also proved that running was the most efficient way to travel long distances within at least one complex canyon system, but nobody knows for certain whether the Hopi actually ever ran end to end through the Grand Canyon. If they did, that sacred tribal secret undoubtedly died with the last village elder who kept it. Sacred trail shrines and ceremonies notwithstanding, what could it have been like for an ancient Native American to run the length of someplace like the Grand Canyon? What was the most practical route for their inner Canyon pathway to follow? When did they run it? And, if they actually did, wouldn't they have had to go in the winter or spring, so that they could run from one reliable waterhole to the next as ancient trails and trade routes traditionally did throughout the arid Southwest?

Perhaps it was all just theory, but these were some of the questions and conjectures that helped me look at the

Grand Canyon from a human perspective. If I looked at it strictly from the standpoint of tackling an inverted Mt. Everest, it seemed so far beyond my grasp that I would have turned tail and run as fast as I could in the opposite direction. But if I looked at it in the light that somebody might actually have done it before—in ancient times—it seemed feasible—not necessarily for me, but for someone. With Tim and Craig standing squarely behind me, I was willing to give it everything I had.

I thought about that as I ran along the historic wagon route marked by the Senator Road. The night was coal black and it was snowing heavily. Huge icy feathers of snow frosted my face and body as I gallumphed through deep, soft snow that buried my tracks almost as quickly as I could make them. It was surprisingly warm for a snowstorm; I could feel sweat drip down my icy neck. Then, winter had just about spent itself, and spring was only weeks away. I was headed toward the headwaters of Hassayampa Creek, the turnaround point for the daily fifteen I tried to burn up and down this historic route in preparation for my inner Canyon pathway. In fact, I'd logged so many miles on this route, which roller-coastered through the pine belt of the rugged Bradshaw Mountains, that I knew it by heart: every twist and turn, every blind corner, the caves, the boulder piles, the deer and javelina trails that crisscrossed it. Tonight, I would have to know it by feel.

That's what I was doing now, running blind through a blowing snowstorm; because maybe, just possibly, there was one last lesson to glean from this experience before I dropped out of sight into forever. Then again, maybe there wasn't. The snow crunched underfoot as I padded along this endless pillow. My lungs heaved in and out, my arms pumped. I sucked in snowy drafts of mountain air, snow-flakes dissolving on my tongue and throat with each deep breath: *hih-huh, hih-huh, hih, hih.* Wild animals couldn't

73

stop me tonight; I felt so good. This was my own stomping ground, and I'd come to revere it in my own way; I only hoped what I'd learned here and elsewhere throughout Arizona could be transposed when I started down my inner Canyon pathway.

I wasn't sure about that, but I knew I was headed toward the site of the old Walker camp, kicking small, white footballs of snow out in front of me with each step. They were a party of thirty-odd prospectors who were led into the Bradshaws by legendary mountain man and guide Joseph Reddeford Walker in May of 1863; the six-foot Tennesseean drove them into the heart of the Bradshaws, after a roundabout two thousand–mile journey, in the hopes of hitting paydirt. They did, and the payoff was beyond their wildest dreams. But even before the big strike, the Walker party had been thankful just to be here. One of the expedition members wrote: "We considered our long journey at an end [at the headwaters of Hassayampa Creek], for at last we were in the unexplored regions of central Arizona, the place of our destination."

When I finally reach the vicinity of their camp, I am covered head to foot with a half-inch layer of snow. The night has somehow grown darker, and I am alone in the wilderness, alone in my dream of running the Canyon. Standing in deep snow at the edge of Hassayampa Creek, the very route the Walker party followed to escape the deadly heat of the desert below, not a sound can be heard except for my breathing. It is as if I've wrapped a downy pillow around my head, because all I can see is the dream of my own journey. Soon I will be running wild through what, to me, is the still unexplored regions of the Grand Canyon. I only hope it will not prove to be my final destination. I don't know, but I'm about to find out.

CHAPTER FOUR

The Abyss

*You must write yourself off before
any big climb. You must say to
yourself, 'I may die here.'*

Doug Scott
Himalayan climber

One moment I am standing on the very edge of the Coconino Plateau, staring into the howling depths of a
fearsome hole in the earth I have steadfastly refused to look
at for an entire year, the frantic wings of a thousand internal
butterflies jangling my nerves raw with a fear I've never
known before; the next moment I am free-falling into the
abyss, plunging downward, out of control, endlessly down,
down, down, as if I'm being sucked into the very center of
the earth. I am. The irrepressible force of gravity has vac-
uumed me off my teetering rimtop perch and shanghaied me
down a crusty trail on the east end of the Grand Canyon,
and it unreels before me like a three-foot-wide-strip of cel-
luloid. Only a triple feature is showing, as I continue falling
down this historic pathway which continues to unwind before me as I chase, in the distance, the thundering hooves of
horses stolen by horse thieves; only now, they're about to
complete a breakneck ride 150 miles across the corrugated
terrain of the eastern Grand Canyon, all the way back to

Utah, without getting caught. Unarmed, carrying but two
bota bags of water and toting a small rucksack that sits on
my back as comfortably as a small squealing pig, I'm trying
to corral that image as the dust stirred up by those long-
dead steeds spins like a tornado into the depths of the Canyon below.

. . . And as I run deeper, and plunge farther, down
these pages of stone that flip past like huge sheets of hard
rock slamming against one another, one synaptic image
fades into the next: that of Manuelito and Begonia leading
frightened Navajos down this dusty path in hopes of escaping the scything, breast- and head-severing swords of Kit
Carson, spinning their own cyclone of dust and terror-
fraught screams.

But they weren't the first, anymore than the horse
thieves were to ride hell-for-leather over the very brink.
Garcia Lopez de Cardenas was, some think in 1540; that's
when he viewed the Canyon as I had only an hour earlier—
before I took this awful, frightful plunge—and determined
the river did not look so far away, as I had. But after three
days of struggling toward that sliver of a river I now see
winding its way through the gaping chasm far below, Cardenas's men Juan Galeras, Pablos de Melgosa, and another
were forced to crawl back out, prompting Cardenas to write
later in his journal: "What appeared to be easy from above
was not so, but instead very hard and difficult." That's why
I've tried not to think consciously about what I am doing. I
just had to step off the edge and jump feet first down the
Tanner Trail in hopes I've beat my fears into the very bottom of the Canyon—the fear of failing at so preposterous an
adventure, the fear of having to crawl back out of the Canyon along the very route of Cardenas's failed expedition.

These are the movies that play for me as I whip into the
stony basin below Cardenas and Escalante Butte, my legs
tumbling wildly, like dice being hurled against the hard felt

walls of a crap table; because that's exactly what this is, a huge crap shoot. And I try to take my mind off these very fears waiting to ambush me by screening Moonshiner, starring Mormon Seth B. Tanner. He rebuilt this old trail in 1889, the story goes, to reach his mine near river's edge. Only later, during Prohibition, whiskey-soaked moonshiners used the old teetotaler's trail to soothe the parched throats of South Rim tourists. . . . And as this movie unreels, I feel as though I'm running into a horizonless cyclorama of the Grand Canyon, against which this endless reel of historic cinema is projected. But this last image dissolves as I slowly regain my composure on this historic spoiler's route.

My two bota bags begin swinging in rhythmic unison to my breathing—*hih-huh, hih-huh, hih-huh*. My footsteps float on an incandescent air-cushion of red dust. My running is effortless, *hih-hih, hih-huh, hih-huh*. I have finally hit my stride, and physically, I feel indomitable. Yet as I streak across the pavement-hard Supai sandstone, I'm suddenly haunted by the stark realization that there may be a very good reason no one has ever attempted this before. But the Anasazi must have experienced this same feeling of insignificance, this feeling of being swallowed alive. How did they deal with it? I don't know.

So I stop a short distance ahead, remove the rucksack, and crawl into a small cave. Carefully, I begin digging with my bare fingers in the powdery red dirt. I'm groping for the straw sandal I know is beneath. I'd found it lying on the surface years ago, and after showing it to my students I'd reburied it out of sight lest another visitor or a scientist abscond with this ancient relic. When I feel the coarseness of the matted straw against my fingertips, I carefully remove the delicate remnant and watch tiny avalanches of red dust spill off it onto my sweaty legs. I stare at it and wonder who wore it, what was he carrying in the crude pack he toted on

a trumpline? Did he run into the Canyon? Did he run out of
it, as the Tarahumara still do in the deep *barrancas* of
Chihuahua far to the south? What did he think about? Did
he have a spirit song he sang for the journey into the earth's
core, so near the Hopi's sacred *sipapu*, "the opening
through which mankind originally emerged"? I don't know.
But holding this matted straw sandal, I know I am no longer
on a historic trail, or even a modern replica of it, but an
ancient pathway that leads to my own. The sandal is more
than that, though; it's tangible, physical proof of what anthropologist Robert C. Euler had written:

> Four thousand years before Major Powell's men tumbled
> through the Grand Canyon in their wooden boats, before
> geologists and archaeologists investigated its lessons and rec-
> ords, before photographers adjusted their focus and tourists
> stood on the South Rim in awe—four thousand years before
> all this, human beings had wandered the Canyon's depths.

They'd wandered the Canyon's depths as I now was,
only I was running through the chartless realm of the Desert Culture and later the Anasazi; in this fragile relic, as
tenuous a link to the past as it was, I had proof I was on the
right path, a path that would ultimately raise more questions than I could answer, a path I knew could take my life
in the flicker of a heartbeat. But it was my choice, my pathway, and I had to follow it, wherever it might lead and
however it might end.

I rebury the sandal, whisking away my footprints with
my sweat-stained bandanna as I step backward; I am erasing
my telltale tracks, so that the sandal may remain sealed in
the red earth, undisturbed for eternity.

I start running again, down this ancient pathway, my
pitifully tiny tracks mere pinpricks beneath the mile-high
wall formed by the Palisades of the Desert to the east. I am
alone, I am insignificant, my movement within this Canyon
is inconsequential to the Canyon itself, to world events

(PREVIOUS PAGE) *Running Paria Canyon,* a principal migration route used by Pueblo Indians circa A.D. 1100. The author ran the length of several Southwest wilderness areas such as Paria Canyon in preparation for his first Grand Canyon run.

Mojave Maze. "The Mojave Indians nearby have utilized the area so marked . . . as a maze into which to lure and escape evil spirits, for it is believed that by running in and out of this immense labyrinth one haunted with dread may bewilder the spirits occasioning it, and thus elude them." EDWARD CURTIS, 1908, *The North American Indian.*

Running the Mojave Indian Trail. Blasted by bitter March winds, the author and Dick Yetman are seen running across the Mojave Sink on the second day of Yetman's unprecedented journey.

Footprints across the Mojave Desert. "No more moccasined feet tread silently upon hard-packed trails whispering *tcawa, tcawa, tcawa.* . . . that a whole mode of transportation is lost, never to be regained." CAROBETH LAIRD, *The Chemehuevi.*

Author retracing the Hopi-Havasupai trade route
across the Painted Desert.

Flint and Steel. The author often used flint and steel to make many of the bivouac fires he relied on to keep warm—and alive—during his long runs, seen here in Cataract Canyon on the Hopi-Havasupai trade route.

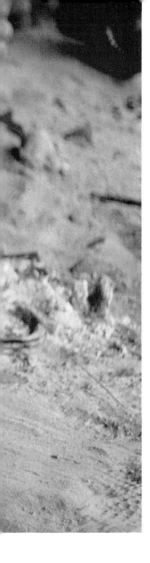

Author face down in a mudhole near Black Falls
on the Hopi-Havasupai trade route. "As you came
around the bend, we heard this gasping—a death
chant. You stumbled over to the water and fell in."
CRAIG HUDSON, support crew.

Struggling through the Kuhni Desert. Dangerously
low on water, the author struggles through the
depths of Moqui Trail Canyon near the end of the
Hopi-Havasupai trade route, what Cushing called
the Kuhni Desert a century earlier.

Rimrocked on the Hopi-Havasupai
trade route, the author and Dave
Ganci look for a way into Moqui Trail
Canyon.

Author (LEFT) *recovering from his near drowning* after swimming the frigid Colorado River (RIGHT), decides to abort his North Rim run . . .

(NEXT PAGE) . . . *until he's reminded of the difficulties* overcome by one-armed explorer Major John Wesley Powell in 1869: "At one time, I almost concluded to leave . . . but for years I have been contemplating this trip. To leave the exploration unfinished, to say that there is a part of the Canyon which I cannot explore, having nearly accomplished it, is more than I am willing to acknowledge and I determine to go on."

m 68.5

being shaped far beyond the South Rim, but at last I am emerging from the dream of running my inner Canyon pathway into the reality of the moment.

Descending the Tanner Trail to the river like a tumbling drop of water, it finally sinks in that I have stepped across the threshold from illusion to what I imagine is real. And what I imagine is real this very moment is that I've fallen a vertical mile within a linear distance of eleven, and my pummeled, blood-gorged thighs tell me I've done it too quickly. But any pain I feel is eclipsed by the fact that I've reached the Colorado River at Tanner Rapids. As benign as the churning waves look to me, I know that they, and the river and natural forces that created them, are responsible for carving a canyon that the best scientific guesses date between 10 million and 1.7 billion years old, far beyond my own comprehension of time and space. What I do understand, dripping with sweat and mesmerized by the ceaseless ebb and flow of the river, is that the Colorado River rises on the west slope of the Continental Divide, near 10,175-foot La Poudre Pass in the Rocky Mountains of Colorado. And, try as modern man has to stop this mighty river with huge, concrete plugs, it continues to flow all the way to tidewater at the head of the Gulf of California, some 1,400 miles downstream from its source. Barely a dozen miles into my own journey, I have reached River Mile 68.4 (measured downstream from River Mile 0 at Lee's Ferry), which I know is another historic milepost. It was here in 1959 that a young boy tried to float the mighty river on a log in a desperate attempt to reach Phantom Ranch; the boy's trip leader had fallen to his death while trying to find a shortcut to the river from the Tanner Trail, and the boy tried to save himself the only way that came to mind. Fortunately, he was rescued before he was swept into Hance Rapids and could contribute to the river's voracious death toll. Before 1950, the *Río Colorado* already had claimed the lives of thirty-

eight people by the time the first hundred people had successfully run Big Red.

Here, at Tanner Rapids, I turn left and head west toward the forbidding entrance to the Upper Granite Gorge;
this is the endless, V-walled tunnel I've envisioned for an
entire year. And temporarily running through it along the
south side of the Colorado River is a heavily beaten path
used by the thousands of river runners who plunge through
the frothing rapids and legendary big drops of the Colorado
River each year. The trail follows the edge of the river
through dense stands of tamarisk trees, which have been
choking the river since they were first introduced to southwest Arizona from the Middle East at the turn of the century. Running through these tammies is to be flogged and
swatted with hundreds of branches and repeatedly jabbed
with sharp sticks all at once. But there is no escaping this
jungle of tammies until I reach Cardenas Creek three miles
farther on. When I do, I'm covered with irritating green
needles and nettles, and showered with tammie dust, and
the salt from both burns the dozens of scratches that
crisscross my body like the fine strands of a red-streaked
spider web.

I stop, remove my pack, and immerse my body in the
frigid river. Historically, the river averaged between 75 and
85 degrees during the late summer, but that was in pre-dam
days. Spewing out of the bottom of Glen Canyon Dam, the
river water at this point now averages between 45 and 55
degrees. And when I sink my heated body into it, I shudder
as if I've fallen through a hole in the ice. I shake vigorously,
screaming all the while, then grab the base of a tammie
before I'm swept helplessly downstream. Revitalized, I drag
myself out and, still dripping with snow melt, shoulder my
pack and bota bags and start running, sloshing in wet shoes
and socks along a steep trail that leads to ancient ruins near
the Unkar hilltop.

Situated on a high bluff, overlooking the bold sweep of
Canyon both upstream and down, this cluster of ruins is
only one of some twenty-five hundred ancient habitation
sites recorded in the Grand Canyon that date back one thousand to four thousand years ago. For me, these small, crude
structures are the next ancient link which connects my inner Canyon pathway. And seeing them fortifies me to plunge
farther into the reality of my dream, but they also pose
a question for me: Did the Anasazi use the same route I
did from the South Rim to reach these stone dwellings, or
did they follow the "prehistoric Indian route going north
from the Tanner Trail over the pass between Escalante and
Cardenas Buttes," a steeper, more direct approach? I don't
know.

But before I run farther along my pathway, I lie on my
stomach, grab the edge of rock with both hands, and peer
straight down to the river boiling through Unkar Rapid
several hundred feet below. River Mile 72.3 is yet another
historic milepost along the river, and I pause a moment to
reflect. On May 26, 1955, Boyd Moore was crossing the
river on an air mattress with Dr. Harvey Butchart when he
fell off and drowned. His pack was later found below Unkar
Rapid, which piles itself in huge pillows of waves against the
arching rust-red wall of Dox sandstone below. Fortunately,
Dr. Butchart didn't let that tragedy stop him. He spent the
rest of his life working out the vast maze of the Grand
Canyon on foot, logging well over 15,000 miles of trekking
in the process. Then, in 1962 a Welshman looked Butchart
up; he'd seen the Canyon, and it so moved him that he
dreamed of walking through it from one end to the other,
but he wasn't sure of the exact route to take. Butchart provided the missing links in Colin Fletcher's dream. Two
months after leaving Hualipai hilltop, Fletcher completed
his contemplative odyssey, and in so doing became "the first
modern man to have gone the whole length of the National

Park [walking] . . . " But when Fletcher, traveling west to east through the inner Canyon, reached the foot of Unkar Rapid, he was able to make his way along the bottom of the wall I was now staring down; the river then was flowing at a mere trickle of 1,250 cubic feet per second. But today the river is so high, to quote Major John Wesley Powell, that it's dashing "its angry waves against the walls and cliffs" below, which has forced me to take this breathtaking detour.

I get up. And with more uncertainty than ever, I start running along this promontory until I can find my way back down to the river on the other side and the route I've planned to follow downstream through Upper Granite Gorge to Hance Rapid. I know this leg of the route I'm following matches Fletcher's, and Tim, Craig, and I have discussed that fact at length. But we think it best, finally, not to compare the two journeys; it would be like comparing apples with oranges. While Fletcher used Butchart's experiences to guide him along each stage of his route, Fletcher undisputedly was the first to tie Butchart's weekend sorties together in one continuous Canyon trek. And while my own route follows in the footsteps of both Butchart and Fletcher, and of others who preceded and followed them both, I am trying to telescope a two-month walking odyssey into a week-long running journey by stripping the adventure down to its lowest common denominator: a lone man, running. We aren't sure if what we are attempting is even possible. And had we not known of Fletcher's successful journey beforehand, we still would have plunged headlong into the Canyon—precisely because of what we don't know and because we are tugged by the same irresistible force that had lured Fletcher into stepping across the brink from his own dream into reality of crossing the canyon on foot.

But this isn't only a dream, because when I reach the river, the route I try following along its edge vanishes again in heavy stands of tammies, deep sand, and slippery ledges

SMALL

of red shale. It's terrain that probably should be walked, but I am still trying to define what is runnable and what is not. So I carry on, hopping from ledge to ledge, drifting in and out of the tammies, slogging through isolated dunes of sand.

I stop when I reach Seventy-five Mile Rapids; it's eleven in the morning and the route ahead is blocked by a series of impassable cliffs hanging out over the river. I'm stuck. If there is an ancient route around this Cenozoic barrier, I don't know it. But I've got to find a way. I have told Craig, when he dropped me off at the head of the Tanner Trail, to wait one hour; if I haven't crawled out of the Canyon with my tail between my legs by then, he is supposed to call Tim to gear up for the next three resupply points, and then begin hiking down the Grandview Trail himself to upper Hance Creek. That's where I am supposed to meet Craig tonight at the first resupply point.

But now I'm faced with two dangerous options: I can backtrack to Unkar hilltop and look for a route high above the river, but that will sap what little energy I have left, if I don't die of thirst along that waterless stretch. Or I can attempt an unnerving hand-traverse along a narrow ledge above the icy river, in hopes I can maintain a more direct route along the river and my only source of water.

The choice is obvious, or so I think. But my mind is so fuzzy from the heat and from having daydreamed through the first couple of hours of running that I don't realize what I've done until it's too late; fifteen feet along a narrow cat-walk, the consequence of falling twenty feet into the icy river hits me. I try to backtrack, but I'm too gripped to reverse the moves. If I fall I'll plummet like a stone with this pack on, and I'll be dragged down to the bottom of the river and trapped in its deadly grip long before I can shed my pack and kick and fight my way to the surface to breach for air.

I begin groping blindly, desperately, as if I'm back on Zoroaster, but each new hold I test breaks off in my hand.

Clinging by my fingertips and two narrow toeholds, I feel myself start to go. The pack and bota bags are dragging me off. I slip, my right leg barn-doors, and I lunge desperately, sinking my left hand in a jamcrack above; it's bombproof. Dangling above the river by a clenched fist, my feet temporarily riveted to a pinch of rock, I squeeze the water out of my bota bags with my free hand and blow them up with air to act as a crude flotation device, in case I peel off. The strength draining out of my left shoulder, I unclip the waistbelt from my back as gingerly as possible, slide off the right shoulder strap, then let the left one slide down to my elbow. Unharnessed from this deadly anchor, I'm ready to move again.

Reaching blindly around the right corner, I pull off another handhold. I try again, more frantic than before; as I do, I slide the inside edge of my right foot around the hairline ledge to support my probe. I stretch farther, teetering, but I manage to latch onto a good handhold; at least it feels good, but after my fall I've never trusted rock like this. Now I have to. But I can't think about the consequences of a fall again or I *will* fall—to freeze and drown like a rat. I release the fist jam and commit to the move; I swing across—and the traverse goes!

I breathe a deep sigh of relief as I scramble back down to the river and trot along the intermittent sand and rock to the mouth of Papago Creek. Here I'm faced with a second airy traverse, but it proves less difficult and less dangerous than the first. Once I complete it, I know the rest of the route to my first resupply won't involve any more climbing.

By the time I reach the mouth of Red Canyon, however, I'm dripping with a nervous, foul-smelling sweat, and I'm dizzy with fatigue. For the first time, I'm having serious doubts about running with a pack on, but I didn't know how else to carry the marginal supply of food and bivouac gear I knew I'd need if I couldn't make the first resupply point in

84

one day. Yet realizing I may be carrying too much weight, I'm reluctant to leave anything behind. ___ חٍٍٍٍٍٍٍٍٍٍ

So I crawl into the sparse shade of a huge white boulder near the junction of the Hance and Tonto trails in hopes of escaping the 90-degree heat. I feel nauseated, too nauseated to eat, and my head feels like a kewpie doll's, spinning in circles, bobbing up and down. The fact that I'm laid up next to the cacophonic twenty-eight-foot fall Hance Rapid makes through the Upper Granite Gorge, one of the legendary "big drops" on the Colorado River, hardly registers. I suck down water, instead, and drift on and off in the same sort of haze I felt when my ankle was twisted back into place.

I dream of Hance, not the rapid—which has become a soothing, resonating background hum surging through the V-shaped glass-black walls of the Upper Granite Gorge—but the man; "Captain" John Hance he liked to call himself. He came to the Canyon from Tennessee in 1883 and rebuilt an ancient trail down the Red Canyon to his asbestos mine on the north side of the river. But Hance soon discovered, as other prospectors had, that there was more money to be made guiding greenhorns into the Canyon than in hauling low-grade ore out of it. As a result, he became the alltime storyteller—if you believed him. Many tourists did, especially those fogbound on the South Rim. That's when Hance would walk up to a group of unsuspecting tourists and say, "Fog's about right to cross." Hance would then lace on a pair of snowshoes, tromp over to the lip of the Canyon, and feel the consistency of the fog with one of his racket-sized shoes; then he'd turn back to the puzzled tourists and say, "It's just right for crossing. But its shorter to the North Rim if I start from Yaki Point. Watch tonight and you'll see my campfire over there." He'd head into the woods then and wouldn't show his face until the next day; then he'd say, "Did you see my fire on the North Rim last night?" If they had, he'd give them a wink and a wry smile; if they hadn't he'd tell them, "Well, I couldn't see your lights over here, either. . . . The fog was pretty thick going over and I made good time. But coming back was different. The fog was thin and it sagged under me at every step. It was like walking on a feather bed and I now feel plumb wore out. Guess I'll take a nap before supper. If any of you folks want to try it, I'll be glad to lend you my snowshoes next time she fogs up good and solid."

That's what I am now hoping for, for it to fog up good and solid, because I no longer feel like running on hard brittle rock. I want to run on the same kind of downy pillow I'd run on during that Hassayampa Creek snowstorm only weeks earlier, even if I have to run it again at night. But there isn't a cloud in the sky, and the sun hammers down on me as I trudge up the Tonto formation through the skull-numbing heat. Situated near the four thousand foot level, fifteen hundred feet above the Colorado River, and three thousand feet below the South Rim, the terrace of Great Basin Desert I am running along begins here at Red Canyon, near the eastern end of Grand Canyon, and ends more than ninety miles to the west. It was this terrace I had envisioned as the ideal inner Canyon route ancient traders used between Oraibi and Havasupai, primarily because it's the broadest terrace coursing east to west through the Canyon. It was also along this seemingly flat bench—what Fletcher liked to call a "hanging terrace"—that promoter Robert Brewster Stanton had envisioned laying tracks for his Denver, Colorado Canyon, and Pacific Railroad at the turn of the century, had he received funding; fortunately, he did not. And all that exists here today is the Tonto Trail, and it slithers its way along the Tonto formation like a headless serpent. I was counting on making a beeline along its scaly back all the way to the South Bass Trail, where I'd pick up yet another trail to link with one that headed down into Havasupai. But today, the Tonto is overrun with feral burros, beasts of burden turned loose by prospectors like Hance, Louis Boucher, William Wallace Bass, and others, the kind of animal naturalist John Muir called "hooved locust." And throughout the long afternoon I run, then repeatedly backtrack, along a confusing network of burro trails that frequently branch off the main stem of the Tonto and end in mindless cul-de-sacs.

There is no fanfare when I struggle into our first resupply point in the blistering sun late that afternoon. I'm totally spent and Craig is stretched out on a foam pad, dead to the world. "Craig!" I whisper. He looks at me, startled, as if he's seeing a ghost; but then, I can't believe what I'm seeing either. We'd planned to rendezvous here, at this tiny pinhead of a spot in the middle of the Grand Canyon—on paper, in theory—but neither of us can quite believe what we're seeing now. It's not that we necessarily doubted each other's ability to reach this point on time, it's just that neither of us had ever done anything like this together before. But here we are, shocked by the fact that we somehow made our first rendezvous point together.

I drop where I stand, and begin rummaging through Craig's pack for a beer. If the Tarahumara, "the greatest long distance runners in the world," spent a third of their time making, drinking, or recovering from the effects of the corn beer they call *tesquina,* we figure we both deserve a brew for our own efforts. I rip open the tops, and hot foam jets everywhere, but we carry our sudsing beers into the shade of a huge cottonwood tree sustained by the trickling water of Hance Creek. $= m 76.5$

Green leaves and clouds flutter together overhead like a skyborn mirage, and I soon lose myself in them, hypnotized by the movement, thirst and fatigue. But I can't stomach the bitter ale, and instead relish drinking the gnat-infested creek water that soothes my feet as the mirage of leaves and clouds flutters faster and faster, my head spinning round and round, until I hear Craig say, "Didn't think you'd make it here today."

"I didn't, either."

"How was it?"

"Craig, it happened so fast, it was like a movie. But it was strange, 'cause it seemed like it took a week . . . know what I mean?"

"Yeah."

But he doesn't any more than I do. It's just mindless chatter, trying to express what can't be said . . . until the clouds and leaves whirl faster, and faster, and I rest my head on the ground in hopes of stopping the endless spinning of the earth. I can't. So I hang on to keep from being swept off.

II

It's half past seven, and the fireball of dawn seems like it burned over the East Rim ages ago; a monotonous veil of gray clouds blots out the sun, extinguishing the Canyon's daybreak pastels. The air is suffocatingly humid, and I feel as if I've already been running for an eternity—*hih-huh, hih-huh, hih-huh*. Endless footsteps slowly nibble away at the Tonto Trail, a mere two-and-a-half to three-and-a-half feet at a time, as if I'm nothing more than an ant-being charging through a boundless crater. I might as well be; my mind is too clouded with exhaustion to accept the fact that I'd run the day before what it would have taken me three to four days to trek. Nor does this curio shop scenery do anything to crowbar me out of my mindless sleep-running: *hih-huh, hih-huh, hih-huh*. My only conscious thought is of linear motion: what will it take to run around the deep travertine drainages that cleave the Tonto formation in five different places between me and the South Kaibab Trail, the next escape route and resupply point to the west? I'm not sure. Cut by eons of headward erosion, these menacing tributary drainages, together with the precipitous, sometimes overhanging subdrainages that incise them, spew seasonal runoff into the Colorado River from the rim-world a vertical mile above. In so doing, they've all but stopped me from making what I'd envisaged in the firelight atop Zoroaster as an arrow-straight run through the heart of the Grand Canyon. Then, that illusion was but smoke and mirrors compared with the reality of following my inner Canyon pathway atop the Tonto Platform, so aptly described by geologist Edwin McKee in *The Inverted Mountains:*

> The airline distance between those places Red and Garnet canyons is not many miles, but the actual travel distance is unbelievably great, for it is necessary to skirt around the heads of innumerable tributary canyons and many branches to each of these. Frequently one sees one's goal a half mile or so ahead but has to travel two or three miles to attain it.

. . . And as I continue heading west, running in and around the unending branches and forks of each of these dark, serpentine moats, a dull stream of images sweeps over me: Craig's knee-wrenching descent down the Grandview Trail to sustain this impossible dream; his lung-searing crawl, cigarette in hand, back up that ancient trail to coordinate the next food drop; his unwavering belief that I'd somehow deliver on my next outlandish promise—"I'm not sure how, Craig, but I'll get to the South Kaibab tonight." These are the images that beat, wisplike, before me as my body continues to move across the Tonto, drawn endlessly, aimlessly, into the depths of the unknown by the magnetic force of the Canyon itself.

The cold fangs of reality, however, lash out at me when I round the western escarpment of Horseshoe Mesa. Coiled like the tail of the devil in front of me is a pink Mojave rattlesnake, a Grand Canyon pink. But before I have time to consciously react, adrenalin has ignited my atavistic fight/flight mechanism. And the next thing I know, I'm leaping over the striking viper. My foot lands; the fangs whip at me like the prongs of a tiny pitchfork; a puff of dust whooshes up by bare leg. And in the very next instant, I'm back in an intensive care unit, at the bedside of my snakebitten sister Valentina. On the brink of death, her thigh is a hideous blue and so swollen with edema that I am reminded of the gangrenous thigh of my dying grandmother. Worse, her calf is a grotesque shade of purple, and her foot has turned a ghastly hue of black. Her toes look like they're about to fall off at any moment, and her entire leg—well, it's really not a leg, anymore—her entire *limb* is oozing with pus-filled lesions and pocked with cavities rapidly dissolving from within by the cancerous hemotoxin of a Diamondback rattlesnake. "Mrs. Annerino, would you please sign this release? We have to amputate." "No, absolutely not."

The strike is complete. The needle-thin, ivory-hard fangs fold back into the viper's mouth. The serpent coils again, and I escape by a breath the horror-filled nightmare of my sister, who hobbled away from her hospital bed with all but a few toes intact.

Rattled awake by this alarming leap, I pick up my pace in hopes of shaking off this haunting imagery as I continue striding endlessly to the west, *hih-huh, hih-huh, hih-huh.* As my footsteps crunch through the coarse sand and hard pea-gravel of the Bright Angel shale and Muav limestone, I try to focus on the tangible physical elements of what I'm doing: the sweat streaming down my wind- and sunburned cheeks like tears from my sister's own desperate struggle to remain whole, sane, and alive; the salt burning my cracked and parched lips; the pasty, spoiled-mayonnaise-tasting saliva coating my tongue; the rucksack whacking against my sweat-slickened T-shirt with an aggravating thump-bump each and every time I take a step; my pathway and how it skirts the crumbly, wafer-thin edge of the Tapeats sandstone, where one broken footstep or one misplaced step means a deadly drop thousands of feet into the Upper Granite Gorge. But the Canyon, the Grand Canyon of the Colorado River, and the omnipotent force it brings to bear on all my senses, snatches away what meager contact with physical reality I'm able to cling to with these thoughts. And throughout that long hypnotic morning, which drags me sleep-running into dreary early afternoon, I feel as though I'm nothing more than a puppet whose progress through the Canyon is controlled by something far deeper than my own cognizant drive to run through the Grand Canyon.

At one time, Cremation Canyon was reportedly used as a vast urn by the prehistoric Native Americans who burned their dead in blazing pyres on the rim high above. And as I stride through this aboriginal boneyard, an eerie unworldliness pervades the scene. I can almost hear the primordial screams of the people as they hurl deathly gray ashes and burnt chips and splinters of bone upon me, showering me with the charred, smoldering remnants of their spirit-kin as I fight to escape the grip of this nerve-bending chasm.

Struggling alone through the sweltering miasmas of this ancient burial ground, I find my pack a burden I can no longer bear. I stop. A zephyr swirls dust around me and spirals up in the hot sun. Whoosh! Suddenly, I'm staring at Zoroaster Temple, across the river, three-thousand feet above. Huddled around that summit bivouac fire, there seemed no better place to view the dream of running my inner Canyon pathway than from the loftiest perch in the Canyon; now, but a pilgrim struggling at the foot of that great temple of stone, I know the reality does not coalesce with the dream, and my efforts to run the loose talus out of Cremation Canyon seem pitiful. Fortunately, I have the Tonto Trail to lead me the rest of the way out, so long as I stay upright, moving. In *The Grand Canyon of Arizona*, George Wharton James wrote: "The old Tonto Trail—the trail made centuries ago by mountain sheep, small bands of which are still to be found in the remoter corners of the canyon, then followed by the Indians, whose moccasined feet made less impression upon it than did the hoofs of the sheep. And in the two or three decades just passed, a few white men trod it," as I was now, running, leaving even less of an impression upon it with my paltry efforts to run a pathway to self-discovery almost a century later.

The midday sun has burned a hole in the cloud cover and I am flaccid with fatigue by the time I reach the junction of the South Kaibab Trail. A major milepost on this journey, this heavily used trail is one of the only rim-to-river trails that didn't follow the natural moccasin-beaten paths of Native Americans or the hand-forged lines of prospectors laid down on top of them. The Park Service chiseled and dynamited this avalanche of a trail into the Canyon in 1925, the story goes, as an alternative to the nearby Bright Angel Trail, because hostler Ralph Cameron was charging a dollar a head for anyone to use his own franchised trail.

Standing here in the middle of the Grand Canyon, festering like a piece of warm bacon left to rot in a skillet, I can easily envision the "gigantic squirming centipede" march of fifteen Havasupai dragging five hundred–foot strands of shoulder-burning steel cable into the very pit of the Canyon, in order to hang the Kaibab Suspension Bridge like a giant gangplank across the booming Colorado River. With some fifty thousand people now piling into the bottom of the Grand Canyon each year, however, the Havasupai weren't the last to test the trustworthiness of that vital, inner Canyon link. The fastest among the new wave of visitors to the inner Canyon, at least in 1961, was Allyn Cureton, who ran like a deer twenty miles across the Canyon, via the North and South Kaibab trails, in a shade under four hours.

I take a long, gagging pull of hot water from my bota bag before crossing this historic thoroughfare, then strike out for Indian Gardens another five miles distant. I know this short leg is the most well-manicured stretch of trail anywhere on the Tonto, not only because it provides hikers with their own vital link between the Kaibab and Bright Angel trails, but because it's presumably the flattest stretch of Tonto between Red and Garnet canyons. It's so level, in fact, that in 1922 Commander R. V. Thomas of the British Royal Flying Corps barnstormed off the South Rim and managed to land his puttering, single-engine plane near Plateau Point, screeching to a stop through a storm of dust fifty feet from the edge of a deadly plunge into the Inner Gorge. But what was a stomach-turning, white-knuckle adventure for Commander Thomas is, at best, dreary labor for me. I'm repeatedly forced to stop and drink in hopes that the hot, putrid-tasting water I carry will stave off heat exhaustion, but I'm hot, too hot, and my thighs are flamed out. So I stumble into the lean shade of a boulder and pass out until I feel strong enough to run a few hundred yards farther. Then I'm forced to sit down again and stare at some blank spot on the ground, my cramped and clammy legs stuck to the Tonto like a fly in ointment. I repeat this debilitating process over and over, until somehow I've covered the interminably long two-and-a-half-mile stretch to Pipe Spring.

I'm met there by the apparitionlike image of Ginny Taylor and, difficult as it is for me to focus, she is beaming ear to ear. In the winter of 1976, Ginny and Chris Wuerhman became the first known modern canyoneers to do below the virtually trailless North Rim what Colin Fletcher had done below the South Rim. It's an enormous stroke of luck to have this lithesome blonde on my support crew, because Ginny has the innate ability to read the scale and weaknesses of the Grand Canyon better than anyone I know. Holding me up, Ginny can't help but notice the signs of heat exhaustion I'm showing. Without letting me cave in to the emotion of the moment, she pumps water down my throat as if she's trying to extinguish a fire—which she does. Shadowing me like an old range hand bringing in a stray calf, she drives me the rest of the way into Indian Gardens, home for the night. I think.   ⸗ ꝳ 89

After Cremation Canyon, Indian Gardens is the next ancient link along my inner Canyon pathway. It was within this oasis of cottonwood trees and perennial water that a small band of Havasupais reportedly sought refuge when hostile neighbors drove them from their homelands far to the east in the Little Colorado River Valley. Even George Wharton James couldn't help but notice the small plots of land the Havasupai irrigated near here at the turn of the century: "This [the Bright Angel Trail]—as were all the trails from the Little Colorado River to Havasu [Cataract] Canyon—was used first long ages ago by the Havasupai Indians."

But any intention I'd had of staying at this historic Havasupai-encampment-turned-Park Service–way station and heliport is aborted, because Dick Yetman has other plans for me. After cracking us both a bottle of Mexican beer, Dick and Ginny push me the next couple of miles to Horn Creek, as if my dream holds the same importance for them as it does for me. There, Chris May, a former student of mine, has our encampment set in the hollow beneath an over-hanging roof of Tapeats sandstone. Chris had learned his lessons well, because he plies the three of us with a sump-tuous meal of quesadillas, smoked oysters, strawberries, and black coffee.

Lying on my back, staring up at the fluted Canyon walls, I'm slowly recovering from the day's struggle, but it's difficult for me to hold back the tears; after two days of struggling alone along my inner Canyon pathway, it seems strange to have what now feels like a crowd of friends pamper me. I couldn't be more grateful, and I sop up their warm, encouraging words well into the moonlit night, which shrouds the Canyon in a lunar mist, as if we're lying on the bottom of a great pool and staring up at the heavens through the water shimmering above. Still, our rendezvous seems more an illusion; none of us seems able to grasp that, together, we're actually running through the Grand Canyon, because it still feels as if the run never really moved from the dream stage to the reality of it. Then, maybe that just isn't possible in someplace like this.

"John, wake up; it's time to go."

I hear Chris's deep voice, muffled, outside my sleeping bag the next morning. I pull the covers back over my head and blot out the Canyon because I no longer want to expose myself to it. It's just waiting out there to take whatever energy, emotion, and desire it didn't suck out of me the first two days. But Chris nudges me again.

"John, you've got to get going."

But I don't want to get going. I know it's late; the heat is already reflecting off the Canyon walls, permeating the thin walls of my nylon cocoon, but all I want to do is stay in this safe, secure womb and pretend I really am not trying to run through this impossible Canyon. I just want to turn the engine off. I feel, as Dave was fond of saying after our Zoroaster climb, as if I've been "eaten by a wolf and shit over a cliff." I'm nauseated, I've got the dry heaves and my left ankle feels like a molten ball of fire. But Chris and Dick literally drag me out of my cocoon. After dressing, I reluctantly start heading west again, along the endless Tonto.

But any freedom of running I'd felt the previous two days is now restricted to a debilitating hobble-run. My right leg, the workhorse of the pair, takes the brunt of the torturous jarring every other step I take. But it's not enough. Each time my left foot kisses the bare rock, a searing pain knifes its way through my leg, as if a saber is being plunged through my heel all the way to my hip. And each time I step, tears roll down my face to merge with the sweat. I hear myself repeating those fateful words in a baleful mantra: "You'll never run again . . . never run again . . . never again . . . "

After six years I've grown callous to this pain that has stalked me through the shadows of my life, waiting to pounce on me and drag me to my knees whenever I step over that undefinable line between joy and pain. And I've proven—to myself, at least—that if my ankle never recovers enough to tackle a Himalayan peak, I can continue to seek my vision and the limits of self-discovery through the wondrous, airy movement I've come to know as running wild. Because I've learned, often the hard way, how to stay out of the shadow world of pain. But this time, I know, I've stepped over that line, and a pain I've never known before has rendered me helpless in the maw of this great abyss.

I cannot—do not want to—continue. It's beyond my capacity to endure. I stop hobbling and woefully consider my plight: What will the failure be like? How will I live with it? What will these friends, who've suspended everything in their own lives to help me, think? Not much. How could they. But before I'm swallowed up by self-pity, Dick nudges me from behind. Reluctantly I take the bamboo cane he offers me and hobble a few more steps. But it feels like I'm running on raw nerve endings, the end of my leg a cluster of veins and arteries dripping with pain, and I stop again. I'm aware of nothing more than this unbearable pain. My pain. Not even the Grand Canyon, in all its scenic grandeur, can eclipse it now. Somehow, Dick knows which combination of buttons to push; he makes a game out of my nightmare by threatening to photograph me if I so much as look as if I'm going to stop and walk. For a while—I'm not sure how long—his threat of blackmail proves too much for my pride and I accept his challenge head-on—until the pain of that saber being repeatedly pushed through my heel cuts me to the quick.

Desperately, I reach out for any thought or image that will dilute the pain. I try thinking of Thomas L. Smith. In 1827, the Kentucky-born mountain man was shot by an Indian while trapping beaver along the Platte River on the east slope of the Rockies. But the camp cook reportedly couldn't stomach the thought of amputating Smith's leg with the swift whack of a butcher knife, so Smith guzzled a bottle of "red-eye" and somehow stayed coherent long enough to cut off his own right leg below the knee. Smith was carried to Green River, Utah, a principal tributary of the Colorado River, where he wintered-up in the care of his three wives, "a Shoshone, a Snake, and a Utah." The herbal concoction they swathed on Smith's stump must have been a miracle cure, because the following spring "Peg Leg" was strong enough to ride seven hundred miles south to the Mexican border. There, Peg Leg and his companion, Maurice LeDuc, headed through "the weird, frightening Algodones sand dunes west of what is now Yuma [Arizona], where the furnace-like heat sucks moisture out of a man's body." Peg Leg and LeDuc led their pack string of stolen pelts west across this searing, hardscrabble desert in hopes of trading them in a small Spanish coastal town, the *Pueblo de Nuestra Señora de los Angeles*. Some historians believe it was in the vicinity of the jagged Cargo Muchacho Mountains that Peg Leg and LeDuc found, scattered atop "three golden hills," a mother lode of black gold nuggets, thus founding the legend of the Lost Peg Leg Mine.

Still hobbling one painful peg-legged step after another, I have little doubt about my own reasons for embarking on my own desert pathway. Should I succeed, which now seems unlikely, the spiritual treasure of having completed the run will somehow erase all the torment and pain

I've ever endured. It will bring new meaning to a life I felt I'd lost after I took the fall. Besides, my pain couldn't possibly be worse than using a hunting knife to hack off your own leg. I only hope, still stumping one leg at a time as I am now, that my gamble will pay off, as Smith's had. *m 95*

By the time I reach Hermit Creek, stumbling, flailing, trying to stay out in front of Dick before he nudges me again, I know I'm going to do whatever it takes to reach the end of this burning pathway, if I have to crawl on my hands and knees to do it. It can't possibly get any worse; it can only get better. I think.

But Prescott climber Brian Gardner is waiting for us at Hermit Creek, and he bears some strange news.

"Tim is skipping the Hermit drop and headed to the South Bass."

Having hobbled and whimpered every step of the way today, it's beyond my capacity to understand that the resupply crew, moving like chessmen atop the game board of the South Rim, thinks I'm going to flash the Canyon even faster than in our most optimistic projections. By way of the Tonto Trail and the wearisome maze of burro trails that stray from it, the South Bass Trail is forty to fifty miles away! Without the Hermit food drop, the South Bass Trail is so far beyond my striking distance it's ludicrous. And Dick knows it. There's only one option; without even speaking, Dick says good-bye and starts running up the Hermit Trail, a cobblestone stairway that climbs a calf-torquing 3,500 vertical feet in seven miles, in the hopes that he can snag the resupply crew before they head for the South Bass. *95?*

Between 1912 and 1930, Hermit's Camp was a one-night stand for dudes who booked passage on Fred Harvey mule trips. For the remainder of the afternoon I soak my weary legs in a pool of slime-green water below this old mule skinner's outpost, wondering whether Dick's gamble has paid off. I know I wouldn't have made it as far as the

Hermit Trail today without his help. And when Tim Ganey and Margie Erhart finally show up at sundown, I know my run would have ended right there if Dick hadn't made a heroic sprint for the South Rim.

With darkness now enveloping the inner Canyon like a black glove, it's far too late to go eight miles farther to Boucher Creek, my original objective for Day 3. So Tim breaks open the first of several six-packs and the four of us pass the evening under the starry canopy of the Milky Way, trying to forget the preposterousness of the mission that's linked us all together. Snippets of conversation sail past as I drift in and out from fatigue: something to do with news releases being fed to *The Arizona Republic* and something about the live progress reports Tim and Craig are giving to D.J. Bill Heywood at KOY, but none of it really sticks. And the next thing I know, Tim is saying, "John, get in the bag."

"Yeah, okay Tim."

A friend from the past, the brother I never had, Tim tucks me into my bag as if it's the most important thing in the world he could be doing tonight. I watch him take a pull from his beer, voices wish me well, and the scene fades to black.

III

The trickling melody of Hermit Creek rocks me awake long before first light the next morning. Peering between the narrow slits of sandblasted eyelids, I'm mesmerized by the twinkling heavens showering the Canyon with stellar dust. Falling stars streak across this canopy of constellations, trailing luminescent tails of silver-white light that arch light-years across the heavens, from the imposing shadow wall of the South Rim over the vacuum of total darkness formed by the North Rim. Yet in the background, I can hear the rhapsody of crickets clicking in tempo to the bubbling cooing of doves in the brittle branches of a mesquite tree. I fumble for my small flashlight as this soothing alarm plays on; I flick it on and begin surveying camp for other signs of terrestrial life. The long, conical beam of light swings back and forth as if perched atop a watchtower, revealing clothes, gear, canteens, boots, socks, and cooking pots strewn about as if our camp had been bombed during the night. Faces squinch out of mummy-style sleeping bags, babes struggling to get out of their own wombs. One by one, I refocus on each of them: Tim, then Brian, Margie, and Ginny. It's obvious that each of them has paid dues to get this far; their haggard, flashlit faces are masks of fatigue, sunburn, and, for Tim, the indefatigable leader, stress. I flick the light off and stare again at the heavens, but it's too late to start time-traveling with Aquarius, the Water Bearer. I don't know what to do. It's obvious that I can't live up to my support crew's expectations, let alone my own. My ankle failed me yesterday, and I have no idea what I'm going to do about it today.

Reluctantly, I wiggle my foot, the same way I've done every morning for the last half-dozen years; there's been no more accurate a barometer than this simple test to tell me what kind of day I'm going to have, whether I'm going to hobble around all day like a gimp and pretend my ankle really isn't on fire or whether I'm going to jump up, click my heels, and dance down the street in the footsteps of Bo Jangles himself. But I don't feel a thing—no pain, nothing! Fearful that I'll awaken the sleeping monster waiting to seize my ankle, I sneak out of my sleeping bag, carefully put my bare left foot on the ground, and stand on it. But the only sensation I feel is the soothing pressure of moist sand and flesh conforming glovelike to one another. I lift my right foot off the ground and jump up and down on my left. Still no pain. I run in place like I'd never imagined I'd be able to do after yesterday's nightmare. Nothing. I slap my foot on the ground, like a paddle being slammed against a Ping-Pong table. Incredibly, the pain has vanished.

I suck in the cool morning air as the first trace of light brushes the fire-hardened black rims of the Canyon from lavender to pink. I want to scream at the top of my lungs and blast the Canyon awake—that I'm whole and complete again! I want to cry with joy. But suddenly I feel the frantic wing beats again, the thousands upon thousands of tiny, fluttering butterflies jangling my nerves raw with fear, because, I now realize, I have forty-five miles of no-man's land to cross by nightfall, the equivalent of the Galiuro Mountains laid down in the heart of the Grand Canyon—only this monumental leg of my inner Canyon pathway will be completely walled in by the South Rim, imprisoning me in an escape-proof corridor formed by the unbreachable Redwall formation on my left and by the black chasm of the Inner Gorge on my right. Beyond Boucher Creek, there's no way out of it I know of until I reach the South Bass, and I simply don't know whether I can run that far in one day after what I've gone through the first three days.

I slip into my running shoes and lace them up like dancing slippers; once again, I crisscross my bota bags across my chest and shoulders *villista*-style. I lash a rolled-up parka (prepacked with rations and survival gear) securely around my girth like the wide leather belt of a bodybuilder. The rucksack I kick aside in hopes that someone will burn it. I turn around and start running, glancing back at the four sleeping bags now squirming in the sand like huge, multicolored grubs. My support crew has no idea what they've done for me, and, today, live or die, I will run for them.

Ten minutes out of camp, however, one of my bota bags ruptures, douching my legs and feet with two precious liters of cold, chlorine-treated Hermit Creek water. But there is no turning back today, not for any reason. I'd decided that yesterday if, by some remote chance, fate smiled upon me today, I would risk everything, burn all my bridges, in an attempt to reach the South Bass Trail, the next resupply point intersecting my pathway to the west. But it represents more than that now; if I have any hopes at all of running my pathway through the Grand Canyon, I have to run this corridor virtually nonstop. So I hastily scrawl a note on a torn piece of map and leave it with the broken bota bag on a trailside boulder: "Bag broke. Don't worry. Feel great. Should be plenty of water en route. See you in church, amigos. Annerino."

According to Tim, the high for the inner Canyon today is expected to reach the mid-90s, give or take five degrees for the Tonto. Still, I'm confident I'll find enough seasonal water en route to the South Bass to replenish my remaining bota bag with the two to three gallons of water I've been drinking each day. That was one of the main reasons Tim, Craig, and I agreed the best time to attempt this run would be late April: nighttime temperatures would be mild enough for me to survive a bivouac in the open if, for some reason, I couldn't make it to the next drop between sunup and sunset, and most of the major drainages would, ideally, still be running with enough residual snowmelt to allow me to run this inner Canyon pathway from waterhole to waterhole the way ancient runners had done elsewhere throughout the desert Southwest—provided my other bota bag didn't break. But I can't be certain, so I just keep running through the golden light of dawn, as it paints the towering walls, the hanging alcoves and flying amphitheaters now encircling me with a warm glow that, in a matter of hours, will turn to searing heat.

As I run, a song plays in my head: there's no stopping it, even if I wanted to, which I don't. It drums me for miles across the Tonto, as if it had been especially orchestrated for this morning's journey:

It is night, my body's weak, I'm on a run, no time to speak, I've got to ride, ride like the wind to be free again.

And I've got such a long way to go, such a long way to go, to make it to the border of Mexico.

So I run like the wind, run like the wind . . .

And so I run, run like the wind, the wind pushing me across a rainbow of joy that now extends from one end of the Grand Canyon to the other, dancing along this spectral arch of light as if this pathway has suddenly been laid down by the glittering wave of a wand. The running is a fantasy come alive; there is no effort, nor is there the faintest hint of pain. It is pure flight. I suck in cloudlike drafts of crystal morning air; I blow out long billowing waves of carbon dioxide across my tongue and lips. My arms swing back and forth, a graceful metronome to my legs, which now fly— bounding, jumping, dancing. *Hih-huh, hih-huh, hih-huh.* It's here—somewhere in the Oz of the Tonto, with the sun now creeping over the Desert Facade on the Canyon's east end, the glimmering silver strand of the Colorado River tumbling and boiling below, the rim-world just hanging there on both sides of me, draping long, flowing sheets of multicolored tiers of stones all the way to the river—that I realize I will have the finest running moments of my life. Because, if I go no farther than Boucher Creek, this incomparable feeling of flight will be the payoff for all the torment, all the pain, I've ever felt; because, now, finally, I'm running wild along my inner Canyon pathway, floating, flying.

Named for French-Canadian Louis D. Boucher, Boucher Creek is a pristine sliver of oasis at the tail end of what was also called the Silverbell Trail in 1891. And for me, there's never been a better place to just sit and wile away the hours, staring at the unending walls of the Canyon sweeping back and forth across the blue sky like curtains billowing in a breeze, than this verdant niche tucked into the folds and creases of the Tonto like some secret passageway. Because it was here that the white-bearded "hermit" "who rode a white mile, and told only white lies" supplemented the meager diggings from his copper mine with an orchard of seventy-five trees, "including orange, fig, peach, pear, apricot, apple, nectarine, and pomegranate," as well as a lush garden, which, according to author Steward Aitchison, also boasted "tomatoes, chili, cucumbers, melons, and grapes." It was here that I first introduced my students to this Canyon wonderland, and it is here that I want to stop and immerse my body in the mesmerizing flow of this rippling creek as it gently winds its way through Boucher's haven down to river's edge a few miles below. But I simply can't. My bota bag is my hourglass, against which time and life are now measured in precious mouthfuls; the sun will climb too high, and the few grains remaining in my hourglass will have drained away if I hang in here longer than a few moments.

I keep running, still flying like a kite held aloft in the wind. But something's amiss. I feel as if someone's staring at me. They are—fellow humans. And when I finally notice them, sitting there propped against orange backpacks, wearing floppy white hats, with little silver cups dangling from their belts, there's a Martian quality to the scene. Not that I didn't expect to see hikers, even in this remote spot a ten-mile drop off the South Rim; it's just that, except for the handful of hikers I saw clustered around the South Kaibab and Bright Angel trails, the inner Canyon has been surprisingly devoid of people. But the eyes of this group betray their collective disbelief that they're looking at a lone man running from where-to-who-knew-where? For a brief moment I'm tempted to stop and explain, until one lady remarks, "Why, what a lovely place for a morning jog." I turn, keep running, and don't look back.

Once I regain the Tonto Platform, I make a mental checklist of the next series of imposing travertines I know await me beyond Boucher Creek: for starters, there are Slate, Agate, and Sapphire; their deep, black, clawlike impressions have been cut through the Tonto as if by the feet of a mammoth dinosaur. Like the travertines of the previous two days, these also have to be run all the way around before I can proceed west again across the Tonto Platform, still suspended three thousand feet below the rim of the Canyon and nearly two thousand feet above the namesake rapids these stark tributary drainages form. Like the Canyon's other seventy-odd serpentine moats, there are no shortcuts around these. Today, however, each of them is an easy mark, and they're all running with water. Still, this is the first day I refuse to look back to see how far I've come— I'm so intimidated by the ground, the distance, and the scale of the Canyon I've yet to run by sundown. More important, I don't want to break my point of focus and diffuse any mental leverage that might be propelling me forward.

By the time I roll into the head of Turquoise Canyon, however, I'm on the verge of "hitting the wall." I'm dorphed out; I can't do simple math without a pocket calculator; I'm hungry enough to eat soap; and my flat feet now feel about as useful for running as the webbed feet of a duck. I start wolfing through my meager rations of two foil-wrapped bean burros in the hopes that the complex carbohydrates will replenish my reserves before I start running again. But before I can swallow the last of this rib-sticking food, my eyelids droop closed. I lie down on the bare ground, curl up like a stray dog, and go to sleep, belching as I doze.

Real and imagined images dance across the backs of my eyelids, but when I finally wrest myself from this ethereal doze, lactic acid has seized my legs and virtually paralyzed them; they feel as if they've set up with cement. Worse, my leaden body has told me that my physical collapse point has been reached. But I have no choice, I have to keep running. Except for the beans still stuck in my teeth and moustache, I have no food. I'm midway across an inner Canyon frontier, and I'm completely locked onto this "hanging terrace" until I reach the South Bass. It's no wonder I suddenly hear Dorothy talking to her dog: "Toto, I have a feeling we're not in Kansas anymore."

I'm not, either. I crank myself back into a standing position and focus my mind on Shaler Plateau, a monolithic, scorpion-shaped buttress crawling across the Tonto to the west. I run toward it. I view it as no more than a visual barrier to run through and beyond. I try not to let any other thoughts or pictures enter my mind, other than the image of a tiny man running, unscathed, through the huge snapping pincers of that red scorpion now poised atop the Tonto.

Tibet's running lamas, or *lung gompas*, once mastered a mystical, psychic running technique called *rkang-mgyogsngo-sgrubs*, "success in swiftness of foot," in order to embark on religious pilgrimages that often entailed running virtually nonstop several hundred miles from shrine to shrine across a 12,000-foot-high wildland called a *chang-tang*. Their point of focus as they ran might be a sacred mountain like 22,000-foot-high Mount Kalias a hundred miles distant. In Alexandra David-Kneel's enthralling *Magic and Mystery in Tibet,* she wrote:

> It is difficult to understand that a training which compels a man to remain motionless . . . in strict seclusion in complete darkness, which lasts three years and three months . . . can result in acquisition of peculiar swiftness. Moreover, it must be understood that the lun-gom method does not aim at training the disciple by strengthening his muscles, but by developing psychic states that make these extraordinary marches possible.

These astounding running monks reportedly chanted a sacred mantra unceasingly until they'd completely disassociated themselves from the physical act of running—to the point, some believe, that they actually were teleporting themselves. Not that I had a clue on earth about how to apply this lost, esoteric discipline to my own running, but whatever slivers of insight I might have gleaned from repeatedly reading David-Kneel's account throughout the long, snowbound Groom Creek winter, and that of Lama Anagarika Govinda's *The Way of the White Clouds,* I hoped would help me form some kind of mental strategy if my body fell apart in the Canyon as it now had.

m 104

I'm not sure where the phrase comes from, or even what it means at the time, but it recites itself over and over until I've fled through the clacking pincers of the Shaler Plateau into the hideaway of Ruby Canyon: "Major domo, major domo, major domo . . . " I'm no longer running; I'm standing, floating outside my body watching myself run, as if the image of my running has been projected across the convoluted walls of the Canyon. I'm hypnotized by this image.

I'm on the verge of hallucinating when this image of running slowly dissolves into the phosphorescent orange glow draping the sweeping Redwall formation that bends around the head of Serpentine Canyon. The sun is going down and tiny white lights are dancing in and out of my peripheral vision. I take that as a warning that I should bivouac before my running floats off the edge of beyond. But dark, ambling silhouettes merge with the dancing white lights; they appear to be threading the narrow Tonto Trail on the far side of Serpentine Canyon, and the nearness of those silhouettes floating across the yawning abyss leads me to believe I can stay coherent enough to somehow reach the South Bass. But first, I stop. I unshoulder my empty bota bag and refill it under a cool rivulet of water. I can't help but wonder if my image of those hikers is real, or if they're merely shadows of stone dancing through a shimmering mi-

m106

rage. I have to find out. I get up and start chasing them. Slowly they get closer and closer, and my image of running melds with their bobbing shadows—until suddenly, I realize they are real; at least I think they are. All nine of them. And these dark shadows hastily go about the worker-bee movements of setting up camp before the last flicker of daylight burns off the edge of the planet. Out of the corner of my eye, however, a lone silhouette breaks off from the others and hovers toward me; a young woman, she appears to be in her early twenties. That's all that registers until she asks, "Are you the runner?"

I nod, then look back up at the miniature cascade of water now pouring out of my bota bag into my mouth. I purposely avoid making eye contact with her, because I'm fearful that if I do, the spell, or dreamlike trance I've worked myself into in order to reach the South Bass, will somehow be broken by the flood of emotions that would come pouring out with conversation.

"You're camped here," she says, "aren't you?" m 107.5

"No, I've got to make it to the South Bass tonight."

Her voice is a warm bouquet of words; my responses seem emotionless, vapid, like the digital voiceprint of a computerized telephone recording. "The-time-is . . . "

"Why don't you stay here? It's getting too dark to . . . "

"I don't have a sleeping bag," I tell her, wondering why I'm now explaining myself to this stranger.

"You can stay in mine," she says softly. Her words hang there, but my mind's playing tricks on me. I didn't just hear that, did I? And for the first time, I look into the deep, dark brown eyes of this dear stranger. In the afterlight of sunset, her soft complexion has a weathered effervescence that comes from traipsing around in the deep recesses of the Colorado Plateau. Her hair is dark brown, loosely knotted in the back, and trailing two long thin braids. Her supple body is firm, yet lithe. And her breasts are cupped-full, molded by a clingy white T-shirt emblazoned with FRIENDS OF THE RIVER. "With me," she says.

But she didn't just say that—"with me"—did she? If she did, I don't believe what I'm hearing or seeing. So I can't possibly answer her. She's simply a wonderful apparition of everyman's Canyon dreamstress. But there it is. Here I am. And there she is. Serendipity and temptation in spirit and flesh, and it's beyond my grasp. I want to laugh. I want to cry. An avalanche of emotions threatens to bury me where I stand. I want to embrace her, and be held fast in her arms by all the worldly security she represents. I want to tell her everything—that, yes, your very presence is warm, tangible, living proof that I'm back in the land of the living after being whisked away from it, myself, by the endless trance-like running through this Canyon dreamscape. But something else is driving me now; I'm not sure what it is, but it's not going to rest until the South Bass is reached. It prevents me from lingering, even for so beguiling a mistress. Or is she? Or is this the same wisplike fox spirit that Buddhist scholar John Blofeld described in *The Secret and Sublime*, the fox spirit who consumed the very life force of a man in the heat of passion? I don't know.

I turn away, not knowing how to respond to that "with me," which is still hanging there in the air between us. The spell is broken as soon as I start running, trying to regain what momentum I've lost during this interlude, before it's lost forever. But I'm in such a hurry to extricate myself from this cosmic union that I almost trip over a backpack. "Excuse me," I say to no one in particular. But once the rest of the group sees that I'm a runner, out here, on the edge of what we all know in the modern world as civilization, they give me a collective "where on earth is he going" look. I'm not sure either. I turn back. The purple fire of twilight burns in her eyes when mine longingly meet hers again, but I keep running. I feel her eyes trace my movement as it fades into night, which is falling now across the inner reaches of the Canyon.

Running, my footsteps probing the rocky surface like feelers twitching in the dark, I remember something I read somewhere, by Haniel Long I think: "The body of man, the body of earth, they may be a part of the same reality." Suddenly, the encounter is but a distant image, and I return to the alpha state of "picking 'em up, and putting 'em down." In moments I am no longer separate from the Tonto. It's taken hold of me, and I'm now physically a part of it as I continue heading on an endless bearing west, my footsteps now tracks lacing a fleeting perforation through the heart of the inner Canyon, only to be swept away by the first dust devil or rain squall.

Out here, running on the hard crust of earth in the cool moonlight, backdropped by a nebulous canopy of stars and constellations, as far removed from everything on this planet as I could ever hope to be, I feel as if I can run all night—I'm so at peace with myself. There is no torment or pain, no exhaustion or fatigue, no thirst or hunger. They, too, are nightmares from the distant past, until I streak down a dark tentacle of a drainage wriggling off the Tonto into Bass Canyon and see what looks like a backpack propped against a rock.

I stop to examine the apparition more closely. One backpack becomes three. What's stranger is that I don't see any sleeping bags rolled out on the ground. I reach out to touch one of the packs to see if they're real. But as soon as I tug the coarse nylon between my fingers, three jack-in-the-boxes spring up from behind a boulder, their heads bobbing and weaving as if on springs: " . . . Annerino . . . ay hey . . . can't believe it . . . ay hey . . . you made it . . . " Disconnected snippets of words floating out of bodies dancing 'round me. Are they real? Or are they fox spirit apparitions? Was *she* real? I look up and see cobalt blue eyes piercing the night; their cigarette-lit neon-blue glow is unmistakable. It's Tim, and I'm home! After building a wall around my emotions for the last forty-five miles, I find myself mauled with affection. Ginny, Tim, and Margie. I start crying. I couldn't ask for a better homecoming.

In 1898, John L. Stoddard wrote: "A monstrous cloud wall, like a huge gray vail, came traveling up the cañon, and we could watch the lightning strike the buttes and domes ten or twelve miles away, while the loud peals of thunder, broken by crags and multiplied by echoes, rolled toward us through the darkening gulf at steadily decreasing intervals"— just as it is about to do to us now.

The following morning breaks cool, damp, and stormy, the buildup of clouds charging the air with such electricity that I can hear a faint sizzling hum as locks of my hair flitter on end. That's when Tim tells me that South Bass Trail between the Tonto and Esplanade formations is too steep and rocky to run safely. Having little idea of the kind of terrain I've already run, I don't push the matter; in fact, the opportunity to visit with Tim during the leisurely four or five miles is too good to pass up. He, Craig, and all the others have expended so much energy supporting this impossible journey that I feel compelled to share the adventure with them. I tell Tim of the trance state I'd run myself into. He asks me about the broken bota bag. That seems like a week ago, I tell him. I mention the Canyon mistress of the day before, but he assures me she was real, that he had bumped into their group coming down the South Bass the day before. But I don't pursue the matter of what might or might not have been said to me—"with me"—because I long to remember the magical moment as just that, as I perceived it at the time, not through someone else's vision.

First climbed by prospector William Wallace Bass

sometime during the 1890s, Mt. Huethawali is a 6,275-foot Coconino sandstone temple. It squats at the junction of the South Bass and Apache trails. When we reach this junction in the drizzly early afternoon, I know I've linked another ancient milepost along my pathway. Originally called the Mystic Springs Trail around 1887, Bass's namesake trail reportedly followed an Indian trail down off the South Rim to Mystic Springs now lost on the outer reaches of the Spencer Terrace. Bass rebuilt the lower section of that path into the Inner Gorge, where he had a cable crossing to ferry tourists across the river to his own orchard up Shinumo Creek. The upper end of the Bass or Mystic Springs Trail, on the other hand, linked my pathway with the Apache Trail; hanging fifteen hundred feet below the South Rim, it interlocked with the rim-top Topocopa Trail that led into Supai. Why it was named the Apache Trail is not known for certain, but it either had to do with the fact that the Apaches extended their far-reaching raids to include the Havasupai in 1884 or with the fact that fear-struck settlers commonly used the term "Apache" for any Native Americans they encountered, and so the name was applied to an old Anasazi or Havasupai trail. But before I can pursue this line further, or speculate on Bass's own experiences when he journeyed along the Tonto east from here all the way to Boucher Creek to visit the hermit in 1887, firebrands of lightning begin drilling the Esplanade formation encircling this ancient junction; and clouds march in over the edge of the Canyon rim like rampaging mastodons. Rain and double-00 buckshot-sized pellets of hail pelt us with stinging sleet. So the four of us dash for a large overhang and hole up to wait for the rest of the support crew.

I drift off as the storm continues to lash the water-streaked escarpments surrounding our stone shelter. But some time later, Tim wakes me up. Chris Keith is standing just inside the overhang; dripping wet, her glistening Shiva smile, the cameras dangling around her neck make her look like she's been sent into the interior to cover a guerilla war. Standing behind her is Chris May; a computer whiz with the mind of a steel trap, Chris May is perpetually feeding the girth of a small water buffalo. Behind him stands lanky Brian Gardner; a cigarette permanently dangling from his mouth, Brian occasionally takes it out to stab the air whenever he discusses existentialism, or Taoism, or climbing, which is always on his mind. Except for Craig and Dick, who unfortunately had to beat cheeks back to the home front, our eclectic group is now gathered. We are on the verge of actually finishing what I knew was impossible before Tim and Craig had pied-pipered the others through this dream. Giddy with food and companionship, the group consensus is that I should finish the run by the light of the moon.

But the weather is not in the good humor we are. Flying white sheets of snow begin drifting ghostlike across the storm-locked North Rim. A bone-chilling rain hammers the mile-high Darwin Plateau. A fierce wind whips and lashes the sprawling, red rock escarpments around us, recharging hundreds of shallow *tinajas* with shimmering mirrors of water. Reluctantly, the seven of us leave the cozy warmth of our lair and slog through the wind, rain, and ankle-deep mud to a series of ledges near 6,400-foot Chemehuevi Point. Swaddled in damp sleeping bags beneath an overhang dripping with an embroidery of rain, we camp for the night so that I'll be in position to start running this ancient track at first light.

It's still raining when Tim nudges me awake the following morning. The ground has turned to mush, and a heavy fog limits visibility to a few feet. In fact, had I been headed to the North Rim in the footsteps of Hance, the fog was definitely "about right to cross." But I'm not, nor is this the break in the weather I'd been hoping for to run the unknown stretch beyond. But it's now half past six of Day 6, and we can't wait a moment longer. Much of Day 3 was spent waiting for the Hermit food drop, and most of yesterday was spent sitting out the weather and trying to catch up on the news. Almost everyone, understandably, has other pressing matters to attend to in the "real world," and for most it will be their last day in the Canyon. So if I'm going to finish what I've begun, it has to be now—abysmal weather or not. I depart. Ginny and Margie follow close behind. The rain does not abate.

If I had been able to trace my pathway across the Tonto with the ease of a sign cutter, the seldom-if-ever-used Apache Trail would become more difficult to follow across the greasy red Esplanade Formation. Where visible, this incipient foot-wide track roller-coasters through steep talus knotted with boulders and brush, and for each yard I gain my left leg is forced to take a sidehill bite out of the soggy talus while my right leg pushes and thrusts from behind. I struggle with this strange, enervating lope, my hot breath condensing in the dewy morning air into steamy puffs, but as hard as I try I can't even out my strides enough to attain a self-perpetuating rhythm of locomotion. Worse, the mud clings to the bottoms of my shoes like dog shit, and I have to fling it off with a kick at every other step.

Fortunately, the temperature is the coolest it's been anywhere along my pathway—in the mid-50s, I'm guessing. The vegetation is more lush; the fog- and rain-glistened pinyon and juniper trees rove across this coral red landscape like fat green bears slaloming in and out of single-stalked century plants. And the trail's position below the very rim of the Canyon, a full thousand feet higher than the Tonto, doesn't weigh on me with that swallowed-up-whole feeling I often felt running through the netherworld of the Tonto, where one misstep would have hurled me to the bottom of earth's own Venus's flytrap.

Barely an hour out of camp, however, it suddenly comes hurtling back at me that I've run this maze before—a year ago, with Randy, on the Arizona-California line, where we crossed the threshold between sunset and twilight by running endlessly back and forth through the ancient Mojave's "mystic maze," a timeless pattern of hand-dug furrows etched into the desert pavement like an alluvial dervish. Renowned photographer Edward Curtis first described this intaglio-sized maze in 1908 in *The North American Indian:*

> In southeastern California along the Colorado River south of the Needles are many mesas, the loose surface stones on the summits of which, covered hundreds of acres, have been gathered by a prehistoric people into long parallel rows. . . . The Mojave Indians nearby have utilized the area so marked, in recent years, as a maze into which to lure and escape evil spirits, for it is believed that by running in and out of this immense labyrinth one haunted with dread may bewilder the spirits occasioning it, and thus elude them.

. . . as I am now trying to do, threading an endless series of fog-shrouded drainages in the hopes of momentarily shaking off the two runners accompanying me. Not that I don't enjoy their companionship; I do. It's just that I was being pulled in two different directions. In the misty horizon of the west I can finally envision the end of this pathway; barring an accident, I am actually on the verge of reaching it. Yet from behind, Margie is tugging me in the other direction: "Come on, wait. What's the hurry?" But I haven't come here to walk; Fletcher had already done that. I came here to run wild along an ancient pathway through the very center of the earth, and now that I am actually about to do that, I am inexplicably torn between these two magnetic poles. Whatever Tim had seen in my eyes that morning, whether it was fatigue, uncertainty, or just plain fear— fear of success, fear of dying—he didn't want to risk having me run this final leg alone, not when we were *this* close. So I went along with his decision to have Ginny and Margie accompany me, "in case something goes wrong," but only because he and Craig have spearheaded such unflagging support in a dream I know is impossible to finish without them.

But as I shift into overdrive to blast across these slick ledges of raw stone, I can't help but feel I'm now running through my own maze in hopes of eluding the spirits occasioning me. Whether they're real or imagined, I don't know.

What originally looked like twelve to fourteen miles on my Havasupai Point topographic map feels more like twenty. And by the time the three of us muck through the mud and cheek-stinging wind to the base of 6,296-foot Apache Point, the weather goes from bad to worse; an unforgiving downpour soaks us to the bone as we struggle up a series of sandstone chutes streaming with rainwater. But the threat of being swept away by a flash flood or being buried under an avalanche of boulders and mud isn't as unnerving as the cacophonous thunder that will blow us apart with lightning if we remain on this exposed ground much longer.

But if there is a trail leading up to Apache Point—and the map indicated there is one—it's escaped our notice; so we stop during our grueling ascent to catch our breath. When we do, we notice five small horses grazing in the stony basin of Apache Terrace far below. They are remnants of the mythical "pygmy horses" once believed to have roamed the western Grand Canyon long ago. The National Park Service conducted an investigation into the matter during the 1930s, however, and concluded that they "were simply Indian ponies, stunted from poor desert grazing." Captivated by this rare sighting, I wonder what it would be like to saddle up and ride out of here in style? Was that the attraction the great Native American runners found so hard to resist after centuries of running, when the Spaniards first introduced horses to the Southwest? I'm not sure, and as tempted as I am to toy aloud with the image of trailing two squaws behind me, I don't say a word to either of my papooseless companions. We turn, face the rain-slickened talus, and continue struggling on all fours toward the natural shelter high above.

Once inside this airy grotto, the three of us clinging like bats beneath the slippery roof of this sandstone belfry, I realize that it offers us little more than psychological protection, since lightning can conduct its deadly currents down the rock's rain-moistened fissures. That fear, along with the image of a mud slide burying us alive, sends me reeling out from beneath this overhang toward the exposed summit of Apache Point. But Ginny's hesitant; if she's one of the premier canyoneers of the day, her Achilles' heel, ironically, is rock climbing. But this is where Margie's buoyant fearlessness and teaching background come to the fore; she patiently works with Ginny, coaxing and spotting her like a gym instructor from below, until the two of them surmount the exposed ground to the ledge I'm standing on.

It's twilight when the three of us reach the crest of Apache Point. It's still raining. The wind is building, now gusting more often than not. And my left knee feels like it's totally blown out, as if I've been hit from the side by a merciless, cartilage-shredding tackle. To make matters worse, there is no cover between us and Pasture Wash, where we are scheduled to camp for the night. Nevertheless, Margie wants to push on, and I go along with her decision in hopes that we can maintain a rapid enough pace to stay warm. But they are fatigued by the strain of tromping in and out of the Canyon to support me; given that, combined with my own stiff-legged efforts, we can't go fast enough. That's when I start hedging. I don't know whether either of my companions has bivouaced in the open before, and with the pace we're maintaining we're not going to reach Pasture Wash any time tonight, especially in light of the fact that we'll have to shoot a compass bearing in the dark to reach it.

Cold, clammy, shivering, I use their wretched appearance as a mirror for my own. I tell them I'm headed back to Apache Point to look for the cave we saw when we first topped out of the Canyon. Margie hesitates, but I keep moving; if she has something to prove to somebody, I'm not playing. This is survival. If the two of them want to keep stumbling in the dark and shiver like dogs all night, I really can't stop them, but I'm heading back. Reluctantly, they turn and join me and we quickly find a small hemispherical cave overlooking the headdress of storm clouds crowning Great Thumb Mesa.

I stare out through the mouth of this cave, but it's now too dark for me to trace the line Fletcher followed around Great Thumb two decades earlier; so I turn my attention to exploring the cavernous interior of our shelter. Erupting from the floor of the cave is a crude stone shrine two feet high; a pearl white deer antler sticks out of its top and a fetish bound with wood and feathers sits at its base. I've never seen anything like this before. But when I look to the west and see silver-blue lightning drilling the base of Great Thumb Mesa with a fire storm of electricity, I can't help but wonder whether this was a power point the Havasupai visited to merge with their spirit world. I am not sure. One by one, the three of us lie down on the damp floor of the cave to sleep, careful not to disturb the area around the shrine. But there has been so much strain today that the three of us shiver independently, too proud to admit to ourselves or each other that we'd be far warmer if we spooned our bodies together.

Images of my pathway, the future, these companions hurtle through my subconscious as I struggle to stay warm, but the mundane images I conjure up fail to provide me even fleeting comfort. But one picture repeatedly surfaces and that's the odd chemistry between Margie and me; I can't explain it, but maybe it has something to do with expectations. Then again, maybe Alan Sillitoe had it right when he titled his classic story "The Loneliness of the Long Distance Runner": that running truly is an intimately private affair, unless you can share it with friends or other runners who know your real strengths and weaknesses, not with someone who will misread your own motives. Then, maybe it's just the stress of trying to survive long enough to see the end of my pathway. I don't know, other than that I am shaking uncontrollably, and so are they. It is so cold it feels as if the earth itself is trembling beneath us.

Something obviously has to be done; if either Ginny or Margie is too proud or somehow misreads it, I can't help it. "Ginny," I whisper, "I'm cold." I snuggle up behind her. Fortunately, Margie takes that as a cue to snuggle up behind me. But the body heat now emanating from the three of us is no longer enough. According to the odd-looking timepiece still wrapped around my wrist, it is a quarter past midnight, and I am shivering like a dog passing a peach pit.

Teeth clattering like spring-loaded dentures and feet stuck on the ends of my rigid legs like cold stones, I roll to my knees and draw my knife and flint. I'm not sure who, but Margie or Ginny gets up and holds the small flashlight as I try desperately to get a fire going before we succumb to second-stage hypothermia. But the tinder I'd hurriedly gathered in the dark before bedding down is too damp; so Margie and I grope in the back of the cave and start pulling apart small chunks of fiber from a packrat midden. I strike the flint again and again against these strange clusters, until the tiny flame ignites the matted clump of hair and twigs and cactus and gum wrappers this family of rodents called home. Slowly, still shivering, Margie and I begin adding twigs, first small ones, then larger and larger ones, Ginny's narrow beam of light spotlighting this meticulous operation of damp, cold fingers stoking what ancient man knew was the miracle of life, until the fire takes, and I finally admit to myself that we're going to survive. And I'm actually going to reach the end of my pathway.

Huddled like hoboes around this life-sustaining fire, bear-sized shadows dance off our bodies and flicker against the walls of the cave. We are warm, and I am happy, but we are stone silent. Whatever our worldly concerns had been earlier in the day, we have since traveled eons together between a sun that never rose and one that never set, and nothing more needs to be said. Because we are surviving the night together, and nothing is more elemental than that. One by one, we lie down again on the floor of the cave to doze in the warm communal glow of our fire; occasionally, one of us is silently summoned from our reverie-filled half-sleep to restoke the fire whenever the cold breath of night exhales through the smoky mouth of the cave. A ceaseless parade of raindrops seeps down along the roof of the cave to drop and hiss on the burning red coals, each drop sending up little puffs of steam and ash.

During one of these somnolent fire-stokings, I notice petroglyphs adorning the moist walls of the cave. Is this the last ancient link along my pathway? Have I finally felt the day-to-day, dawn-to-dusk struggle of the ancient Native American runners singing a spirit path? I lie back down, too tired to answer my own question, but my closed eyelids are now a window to the past. Through these panes I watch fleet-footed, sticklike shadows running through the desert, singing mythical spirit songs in a high-pitched whine as they stride, drums beating to their footsteps, into their ancestral hunting grounds. Whether or not I've been able to relive that vision along my own pathway, I can now see a lone figure following in these Canyon runners' footsteps in the great Mojave Desert to the west: a wind blows across that fearsome land, inflating a brown wall of dust that envelops the horizon in the four cardinal directions. Running head-on toward the storm, this tiny silhouette embraces the dreamy wall of dust and disappears. The only seeing in this monstrous cloud is feeling: parched lips, a throat choked with thirst, a face streaked white with salt, eyes peppered with sand, legs slick with sweat. Finally, the silhouette emerges from that colossal airwave of sand to burn across the desert pavement into the eternal horizon where there is no ego, only the movement some call running.

When I peer out through the mouth of the cave early the next morning, the Canyon is still shrouded in a foggy mist. But that's all I can see: white clouds, rimmed by the dark orifice of the cave entrance. Suddenly I'm reminded of a passage from Lama Govinda's book *The Way of the White Clouds:* "There are mysteries which a man is called upon to unveil, and there are others which are meant to be felt but not to be touched, whose secrecy must be respected." And now, as far as I have followed my inner Canyon pathway in both reality and in dreams, other voices are asking me to do just that—respect the secret: finally it hits home that I can't follow my pathway into Havasupai as I've dreamed of doing for so long.

That's what Tim had told me the night I strode into the South Bass drop. But I was so excited and dorphed out and confused that I ignored it when he said, "John, you can't run to Supai." In fact, I'd ignored it all the next day, and the day after that, because I knew it would take whatever con-centration I had left just to reach Apache Point, where I could literally fall the rest of the way down the Topocoba Trail into Supai. What an ending: a virtual free-fall into the heartland.

So I really haven't given it much thought until now, as Ginny, Margie, and I crawl out of our cave into the swirling white clouds, wondering which way to go from here—east to Pasture Wash or west to Havasupai? I am torn again, because Supai is the only place to end this pathway, at the very village to which Hopi traders had traveled from the east and to which the Mojave had traveled from the west. But I'd have to run those last fourteen wonderful miles as an outlaw because the Topocoba Trail, used by Fray Francisco Garcés as early as June 25, 1776, is now part of the Havasupai's "traditional use area." Not even Colin Fletcher had had to face that obstacle when he followed his magic line around Great Thumb Mesa right through the soul of the Havasupais' sacred land. But these are different times, and whether there is any historic or spiritual insight to be gleaned by following my pathway the rest of the way into Supai, the Topocoba Trail is now off limits to all but Native Americans. Even were I tempted to, there has been too much boldface ink and too many glowing radio dispatches for me to run it surreptitiously. The brain trust at the Grand Canyon Backcountry Ranger Office has told Tim that if I run to Havasupai anyway, there really is nothing they can do to stop me. But they also told him, in no uncertain terms, that that might ruin the already tenuous relations between the National Park Service and the Havasupai tribe, so that this "traditional use area" will remain off limits to Anglos forever. And I am not the one to close that door.

Reluctantly, I turn east/southeast at Apache Point and begin stumbling through the mud, sagebrush, and juniper toward Pasture Wash Ranger Station, fifteen miles cross-country by compass bearing. But this "running back from the end of my run" proves to have the most difficult footing of the entire route. And I try not to cave in to the thought that running to Supai would be so much easier and so much more spiritually fulfilling, because that's where ancient traders went, not to a government way station.

. . . but as I continue flailing through the sagebrush, which covers this burned-out, overgrazed land so densely that it tears at my legs from the knees down, Margie and Ginny cheer me tirelessly from behind. I feel more an old man who's been chasing windmills than the "conqueror" the headlines are already making me out to be.

But the dream is behind me now, and whether it ever evolved into reality I never was completely certain, because the threshold between the dream of running my pathway and the reality of it was so permeable that it couldn't be grasped, any more than I could hold water in my fist. And what yawns before me is a feeling of emptiness, as if my life force has been so completely swept away by the Canyon that I have nothing more to give to it—or anybody or anything else, for that matter. I feel as if I'm running through a spiritual void as vast and as awesome as the Canyon itself.

. . . but should I forsake this Canyon, as I promised myself I would if I didn't perish along my pathway, I now realize that this feeling of emptiness will remain within me forever, as cold and as lonely as any bivouac. The pathway will remain not something tangible that I can hold, cherish, or even point to—"Yes, one day I followed that path"—but a wisplike fantasy of one romantic's pitiful attempt to master his fears and emotions by running through the heart of the Grand Canyon. All because the Canyon—the beautiful, godforsaken Grand Canyon—remains unmarked, as if I hadn't wept and crawled, run and struggled my way through it. And because it would remain out there on the edge of my day-to-day existence beckoning me, teasing me, luring me like that quintessential fox spirit, taunting me that I'd left the frontier of my soul unexplored.

. . . and if ever I am to fill the stark void I now feel as the three of us lunge toward a parking-lot press conference—the South Rim celebration—I know, as I feel and taste the tears streaming down my sunburned cheeks, that I will have to embark upon the shadow legs of my pathway too: the rim-bound ancient path of Hopi-Havasupai and the savage arena of the North Rim. Then I will have to consider them both, train my heart out, and finally, I will have to abandon each leg as utterly impossible—until that is, I can no longer stand the taunting and, trembling once more with the greatest fear I've ever known, wrap a scarlet bandanna around my head and try running for a few eternal moments in the spirit tracks of those who ran before me.

CHAPTER FIVE

Lessons from the Ancient Path

No more moccasin feet tread
silently upon hard-packed trails
whispering tcawa, tcawa, tcawa . . .
a whole mode of transportation
is lost, never to be regained.

Carobeth Laird
The Chemehuevi

In the cold, blue light of dawn the wind snaps and twists in snarling gusts, blasting us with the bitter winds of March as the two of us run for daylight across the Mojave Sink. But for every step we take, these merciless headwinds sheer us raw with chills as we struggle across this horizonless salt pan toward the Devil's Playground. We've been following the pulse of the Mojave River, which flows through a subterranean chamber far beneath the sere white crust of this dry lake, for more than a day; and now that the "upside-down river" has finally dumped its heart out here in the middle of the Mojave Desert, these chest-pummeling winds threaten to slam us back two steps for every step we punch forward. But we feign from right to left, and bounce and weave like pugilists shadowboxing with a force we can neither see nor

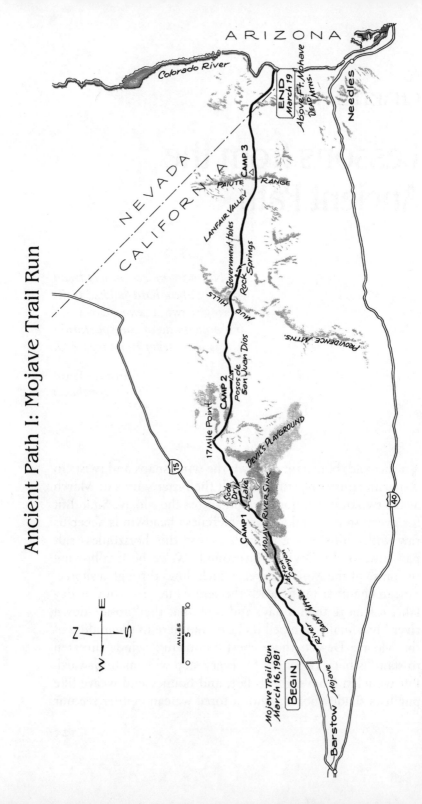

Ancient Path I: Mojave Trail Run

ARIZONA

Colorado River

NEVADA

CALIFORNIA

Needles

END
March 19
Above Ft. Mohave
DEAD MTNS.

CAMP 3

PAIUTE RANGE

LANFAIR VALLEY

Government Holes

Rock Springs

MID HILLS

PROVIDENCE MTNS.

CAMP 2

Posos de San Juan Dios

17 Mile Point

DEVILS PLAYGROUND

Soda Dry Lake

CAMP 1

MOJAVE RIVER SINK

15

40

Afton Canyon

CADY MTNS.

MOJAVE RIVER MTNS

Mojave Trail Run
March 16, 1981

BEGIN

Barstow Mojave

N
W — E
S

MILES
0   5   10

Drawn by Michael Taylor

reckon with; it hammers us from all directions, and I wonder how soon this furious beating will leave us sprawled face down on the salt-caked mat of Soda Lake. Not the idyllic conditions we'd first imagined when we set out to cross the Mojave Desert before the summer sun ignited a blazing inferno, but conditions are seldom ideal for man in an environment that has existed for eons without him.

The ageless path we're tracing once connected the Mojave villages on the lower Colorado River with those of the Gabrielinos and Venturenos near the Pacific Ocean three suns west. Traversing more than three hundred miles of sand, dry lakes, lava flows, boulder-strewn washes, and mountains that erupt out of the earth's fiery core as if the Mojave themselves had etched them on this ancestral-scape, the Mojave Indian Trail links a necklace of precious waterholes westward across this uninhabited waste until it reaches Soda Lake, or the Mojave Sink, which drains the very heart of this desert. Moving, as anthropologist Al Kroeber wrote, "across the country in a trot that carries them over long distances rapidly," the Mojaves ran west from Soda Lake, along the course of their namesake river a hundred miles to its source, which tumbles out of the great divide cleaving the San Gabriel Mountains from the San Bernardino Mountains to the east. It was through this mountain passageway that the Mojave ran in order to visit and barter with coastal tribes in the heyday of ancient traders.

For most starry-eyed immigrants who later followed in the Mojaves' footsteps along this desolate leg of what was also called the "Spanish Trail" during the 1850s, North America's smallest desert proved to be everything but the promised land they'd envisioned on the west end of it. But to people like the Mojave, who were known to run a hundred miles a day along this prehistoric track, it was mythical running country, just as it was for their symbiotic neighbors, the Chemehuevi, whose own running prowess knew only the limits of their territorial hunting songs.

As we run through winds that cuff us around like a great bear pawing at a couple of field mice, the Mojave Desert still is as mythical a running country as I can imagine. The timeless path now guiding us across it tugs us into a holocaust of fire mushrooming out of the eastern edge of our cold planet. But soon, I know, the Mojave Indian Trail will cross the song tracks of the Chemehuevi, who sang and ran their way across their own spiritland, guided only by their ancient songs, which bound a sacred link between them, this desert, and the very quarry they hunted. In her eloquent book, *The Chemehuevi*, linguist Carobeth Laird wrote:

> . . . even in the closing decades of the nineteenth century, there were still some groups of as many as twenty-five or thirty men inheriting the same song and hunting range. When a Chemehuevi asked, 'How does that song go?' he did not refer exclusively to its words and tune; primarily he meant, 'What is the route it travels?' Each landmark and watering place was mentioned in order, by recognizable allusion or description if not by name, so that a man's song constituted an oral map of his territory.

Songs like the "Route of the Southern Fox" flashed out of the heartland of the Chemehuevi more than two hundred miles north to Death Valley, called *Kunayiwaavi*, Fire Valley, because the body of the fox "was consumed by fire until only his head remained." The free-roaming "Salt Song" flew in around the desert and mountains squeezing the Colorado River like the wing beats of that primal song track.

Beyond the Chemehuevi's own songs and trails, however, the Mojave Indian Trail was only one leg of a much larger trade route that wound its way east from the Pacific Ocean, across the Mojave Desert, along the edge of the South Rim to finally link up with the Zuni Pueblos in the territory of New Mexico. It was along this desolate, 1,100-mile-long track that the Mojave, Walapai, Havasupai, and Hopi traveled to each other's distant villages to trade seashells, deerskins and desert bighorn sheepskins, woven goods, pottery, and other small, easily transportable goods. Some tribes acted as middlemen for one another, and tribes like the Mojave reportedly ran as much for the adventure of visiting distant territories as they did for the benefit of trade. What was it like to actually follow a leg of this great trade route? Could the land still be seen through running as the Mojave and Chemehuevi had if one followed in their exact footsteps? I'd dreamed of finding out.

Not long after staggering away from the South Rim a year earlier, I knew it was feasible for ancient runners to have run through the heart of the Grand Canyon, but I wouldn't know how practical it would have been for them unless I compared my inner Canyon pathway with the rim-bound trade route. And the best place to start, I first thought, was not the shadow pathway of the Hopi-Havasupai leg, but out here at the beginning—or near the end—of this trade route where the ancient path could still be followed on the ground. However, I was beginning to stack the deck against myself, because I was intent on leaving the Oraibi sometime in April, before summer blistered the *Desierto Pintado* (Painted Desert) and the Coconino Plateau into an oven of death for any runner; that meant I'd have to slide the Mojave Indian Trail into March, and I simply didn't know if I'd recover soon enough to embark on the Hopi-Havasupai Trail. Dick Yetman realized that much sooner than I did and earnestly went about making plans to run the Mojave Indian Trail while I was still researching it; and if, in a moment of weakness, I was miffed that this pathway might soon be run by someone else, I knew I couldn't run both pathways back-to-back. So I eagerly fell back into support position in hopes that I could help Dick see his pathway to the end, as he had done for me. Besides, the rim-top Hopi-Havasupai Trail would come closer to proving or disproving my inner Canyon hypothesis than would the Mojave Indian Trail.

Then, that's where the two of us are now—almost forty miles into a hundred-and-thirty-mile-long track that, during the summer, burns across the Mojave Desert like a smoldering dynamite fuse. But this March wind, blowing out of the depths of the Grand Canyon two hundred miles east, threatens to snuff out Dick's own burning desire to reach the Colorado River ninety miles away, even as he continues to bob and weave his way across the Mojave Sink into sunrise of Day 2; in the gold-blue light of dawn, Dick is still jabbing at forces most travelers contended with more than a century before. The first non-Indian to actually thrive on this prehistoric trail, however—as well as to travel the entire trade route east to the Hopi villages—was Spanish missionary Francisco Tomás Garcés; he crossed the Mojave in February of 1776. Somewhere in the vicinity of the Providence Mountains, which the Chemehuevi called the Green Stone, he met a group of Mojave, most likely runners. In his diary, Garcés wrote:

> Here I met four Indians who had come from Santa Clara to traffic in shell beads. They were carrying no food supply, nor even bows for hunting. Noticing my astonishment at this, where there is nothing to eat, they said, "We Jamajabs can withstand hunger and thirst for as long as four days," giving me to understand they were hardy men.

So is Dick. As we crunch across the broken-eggshell surface of Soda Lake, which Garcés's historian Elliot Coues himself crossed a hundred years before us, the pummeling winds finally subside with the rising sun, and I suddenly feel hungry enough to eat a horse, or at least part of one. Then that's exactly what Kit Carson and his party of trappers were forced to do when the mountain men crossed the Mojave Desert in the winter of 1829. Wrote Carson: "We met a party of Mohave Indians and purchased from them a mare, heavy with foal. The mare was killed and eaten by the party with great gusto; even the foal was devoured." But Dick is running so strongly now, like the Jamajabs Garcés met two centuries earlier, he seems impervious to hunger and fatigue. And it's only with tremendous effort that I'm able to slingshot far enough ahead of him to frame him with my telephoto lens before he tramples over me and the lion now growling in the pit of my stomach.

Chris Keith and I have been alternately shadowing Dick since leaving the historic military outpost of Camp Cady the dawn before; we figured that was the best way to document his pathway, by running every other stretch of it with him. Covering only half the distance he ran was the easy part. The hard part was following this ancient path across a 40,000-square-mile desert, and that would have been like looking for a contact lens in a cantina full of broken beer bottles were it not for Mojave Indian Trail historian Dennis Casebier. The trail was first described in Garcés's own diary, translated and annotated by Elliott Coues in *On the Trail of the Spanish Pioneer,* but no modern man knew exactly where the Mojave Indian Trail lay until Casebier sauntered into the mind-alternating puzzle of the Mojave Desert. It was a labyrinth that took the physicist twenty years of gumshoeing through the National Archives and other records—and who knew how many trips to the eastern Mojave—before he actually pieced the Mojave Indian Trail together, on foot.

In *The Deserts of the Southwest,* Peggy Larsen wrote: "The desert holds a mystique, a subtle fascination, which is difficult to pinpoint and even more difficult to describe. Not all people are so affected by it, but those who have experienced the desert in this way are the richer." Casebier was so affected by it that he wanted to see the Mojave Indian Trail eternally preserved, possibly as a National Historic Site. And he hoped that if Dick were successful it might bring him a hair closer to fossiling this pathway for future generations to explore. So Casebier sent along a cassette tape describing in exacting detail how to stay on the trail, and where to look for it if Dick wandered astray. Before each leg of the run, Dick would play this tape for Geary Redmond and Jim Gaston, his handpicked support crew, so they'd know exactly where to pinpoint the midday checkpoints and evening campsites. Wrestling with windblown topographic maps in the middle of the desert, I found it strange yet comforting to listen to the distant voice of this master puzzle-solver: "Here we are at what I suppose is the most dangerous part of the trail . . . so take out your Cave Mountain quadrangle." Squatted like aborigines around the tiny recorder, we hung on his every word—as if fate, itself, hinged on them.

But even with Casebier's tape and our topographic maps lined with felt-tip tracks guiding us from waterhole to waterhole, some relic stretches of the Mojave Indian Trail can't be followed in situ, simply because they've been engulfed by sand or recklessly devoured by ORVs. So once Dick and I emerge from the salt-encrusted rim of the Mojave Sink, we strike out cross-country for Seventeen Mile Point. Fortunately, the wind has turned back on itself, and it's now chasing us through the desert like bands of Mojaves who, historians tell us, sometimes preyed upon wagon trains to supplement their meager rations of lizards, screwbeans, and maize. This stammering run ends, however, as soon as we enter the mine field of rodent sinkholes Casebier had warned us about. Every few minutes, one of us plunges into a knee-wrenching explosion of sand and saliva, struggles out, only to drop like a bomb again another fifty to seventy-five yards downwind. As frustrating as this bombing run is, however, it's difficult to hold back the laughter every time one of us misreads this crater-pocked footing.

I'm still wondering if the Mojave runners didn't somehow teleport themselves over this field of sinkholes when we finally reach Seventeen Mile Point. It's 9:00 A.M., the Mojave wind is now breathing down our backs, and my knees and ankles feel as if they've been staked to the ground. Dick, on the other hand, is a picture of stalwart determination, conjuring images of a tireless frontier scout leading the great migration of wagon trains west along this 35th Parallel route in pursuit of Manifest Destiny. Suddenly, however, I'm confronted with two vehicles from Dick's support crew; while I eagerly greet Jim and Geary's hearty welcome, their fossil-fueled wagons temporarily whisk me away from a path that once only whispered of footsteps dancing in sacred communion with the earth, long before it was churned to dust by the ceaseless grind of wagon wheels.

POZOS DE SAN JUAN DIOS
On March 8, 1776, Fr. Francis Garces, OFM,
On his most famous journey of
Over 2,000 miles from Mission San Xavier
Del Bac, Tucson, Arizona, to
Mission San Gabriel, California, rested
here and named these waterholes
"St. John of God Springs," (Marl Springs),
and on the return journey
Passed through here, May 22, same year.

At sixty-six miles out, Pozos de San Juan de Dios marks the halfway point on Dick's pathway to the river. And by the time his silhouette floats out of the steamy horizon of lava and cinder cones on the fringe of the Marl Mountains, he says he "can hear wagon wheels on rocks and the snorting of horses." Then, the voices Dick hears echoing from the past may be those of the Whipple Expedition, whose Pacific Railroad Survey churned through Marl

Springs on March 9, 1854. Expedition quartermaster Lt. David S. Stanley wrote that he thought the Mojave Trail was "unfit for wagon road or for pack mule trains. . . . Had we not had Indian guides, well acquainted with the country, we would have certainly lost all our animals, if not men." Whoever Dick hears talking to him, it is becoming more and more apparent that, like the Chemehuevi, he is finding his own connection with the land.

But there are other forces at work out here besides the phantom wagon trains. Winter light refracting off this desert mirror by the low-angle track of the sun magnifies distant mountains as if they are submerged in a crystal pool of water, which makes them seem larger and closer than they really are. Eighty miles to the north, the Panamint Mountains form the west wall of Death Valley; to the Chemehuevis, this range was "sacred land, the Storied Land, where the great myths were said to begin and end." A hundred miles to the south, however, the snow-dusted San Jacinto Mountains clutch longingly at the blue heavens; naturalist John Muir remarked that the view from the summit of that 10,804-foot range was "the most sublime spectacle to be found anywhere on this earth."

As Day 2 draws to a close at this historic waterhole, the four of us watch Dick streak toward camp. The sight of a lone man running his pathway through a desert marked by the Storied Land to the north and "the most sublime spectacle on earth" to the south stirs such deep atavistic impulses, I can't help but believe that running is simply the most practical way to cross this mythological region bounded only by the spiritual wanderings of man.

In *The Chemehuevi*, Laird also wrote: "In the last two decades, they (the Chemehuevi) ran simply for the joy of running in each other's company, taking the old trails well back from the River." As I cradle a metal cup of hot coffee next to a small fire on the crisp dawn of Day 3, it's easy to grasp the vision Laird spoke of. Chris and Dick are sticklike silhouettes floating on the horizon toward the Mud Hills and the Providence Mountains. These ranges were traversed not only by the free-roaming Mojave, but also by the Chemehuevi, whose own running paths crisscrossed those of the Mojave near here while following their ancient spirit songs. In moments, the tiny Stick People disappear into the shimmering mountain wall, and through my telephoto lens they appear to have transcended the physical act of running on a pathway back through the ages of man, when a mile was determined not by distance but by the stark features of this land.

To the Chemehuevi runners, according to Laird, a mile was "the land from the top of one mountain range, through the intervening valley, to the top of the next mountain . . . literally, one desert." It takes the Stick People most of the morning to run one and a half *cuukutiiravi,* or Chemehuevi miles, from Pozos de San Juan de Dios, through the cool spring desert, over the snow-flecked Providence Mountains, to Government Holes. Jim, Geary, and I rendezvous with the Stick People there. But the tenacious Mojave wind blows right through them, rattling their brittle bones with cold; so Dick runs one last "white man's mile" alone to the shelter of Camp Rock Spring. Seen through the long lens of my camera, the Stick Man is still running as if yesterday had never happened and tomorrow will never come. But the loose footing has torqued and wrenched his tendons and joints, and the Stick Man begins favoring his left leg; and each step that gobbles up a tiny piece of the horizon also mirrors the pain of my own inner Canyon pathway.

By the time the Stick Man dances with the petroglyphs at Camp Rock Spring, however, he's stormed through that wall of pain and I realize he's going to do whatever it takes to reach the end of his pathway at river's edge. Once known to the Chemehuevi as *Tooyagah,* "Center of the Pass or

Boulder Pass," this prehistoric waterhole was also important to the mountain men, immigrants, prospectors, and explorers who crossed this hard desert in the hopes of reaching the Mojave River without perishing of thirst. In April of 1984, Lt. John C. Fremont painted his own vivid picture of how white men viewed travel through this ancestral desert:

> Between us and the Colorado River we were aware that the country was extremely poor in grass, and scarce for water, there being many *jornadas* [day's journey], or long stretches of 40 to 60 miles, without water, where the road was marked by bones . . .

By noon, I'm straining at my halter to start running the next *jornada* with Dick, but his legs have, understandably, fatigued since leaving Camp Cady eighty-six miles earlier. He soaks them in a cool mudpack while I pace around in the background waiting to be unhobbled. Two hours later, Dick's earthen remedy seems to have done the trick, and we trot down the gravel bed of Watson Wash until we can break out of it and head cross-country; once we do, though, we are confronted by a dense forest of cholla cactus. There is no trail through this menacing stand of "jumping cactus," so we begin hunting for a way through it without getting peppered by needle-covered cluster-balls. Only then will we be able to concentrate on relocating the Mojave Indian Trail.

It's at this point in the journey that I begin to realize Dick's pathway is as much a geographical puzzle as it is a transtemporal adventure. Ancient paths that tracked the Southwest had one of two distinct characteristics. They were either so well trod, and so preserved in the dry soils of the desert, that you could still follow the exact path of the ancients, as was generally the case of the Mojave Indian Trail, or, like the Hopi-Havasupai Trail, because of its wetter climate, higher elevation, corresponding life zone, and topography, only its basic route of travel could be followed from one geographical point—a prominent hill, mountain, river, pass, etc.—to the next.

Having unimaginably slipped through this savage cholla forest without being punctured by a single pincushion of anteriorly barbed, needle-thin arrows, we put our noses to the ground and zigzag back and forth like a couple of blood-hounds until we find the trail just about where Casebier said we might: "When you get over there about where the map says 4660, you're gonna have to find the trail there or you probably won't find it most of the way across Lanfair Valley. It's not really a trail, it's a ditch." We hop down into this ancient path, which has been worn so deep by the heavy iron-rimmed wheels of eight-mule-team wagons that it now acts as a storm drain for monsoon runoff, and start running below the level of the ground. Our eyes peering a few feet over the edge of the desert sliding past, we beat cheeks for Lanfair Valley seven miles distant.

But sitting there in the heart of this sprawling valley is the strangest sight I've ever seen in this desert, or any other: a telephone booth! There's not a building in sight for miles around; there are no signs, or survey stakes, or any other clue that some eastern developer had a hallucination about building a casino or resort community in the middle of this Hidden Quarter, just sage, Joshua trees, a few lizards trying to stir up a little excitement with their afternoon regimen of pushups—and a telephone booth. Dick and I rendezvous with his support crew in this Twilight Zone, otherwise known as Lanfair #1, then push on toward Paiute Springs.

We're not a half-hour out from this water stop, how-ever, when I realize we're running through the desert's own magic time, when its natural forces shape your running, your perceptions, your vision. Shadowing each other side by side, we hammer our pace, but we can't run fast enough now. We gulp double drafts of air, blow in and out like tom-toms: *hih-hih/huhhh, hih-hih/huhhh, hih-hih/huhhh, hih-hih/huhhh, hih-hih/huh.* Our footbeats trammel a staccato beat, whispering a *tcawa-tcawa, tcawa-tcawa, tcawa-tcawa, tcawa-tcawa.* We are no longer running; we are gliding, and we can't slice the ground fast enough: *hih-hih/huhhh, hih-hih/huhhh, hih-hih/huhhh.* . . . And the farther we slide toward the Paiute Mountains, bristling in the distance like a huge porcupine crawling across the landscape, the more shadowlike we slip through the sizzling orange luster now blanketing the desert. There is no identity now. Inner dialogue is still. Desires and emotions no longer exist. There is only the feeling of flight. Stick Men streaking through the palpitating orange specter of late afternoon until it swirls through the amber light of sundown and embraces the soft luminescent blues of twilight. Gray fades to black, and the incipient path is lost in a maze of braided washes.

In the distance, a full moon climbs over the porcupine range, showering the Paiutes with a brilliant cold-blue lunar dust as dual shadows run toward the craters of the moon. A feeling of bewitchment transcends this aerial pathway, and the entity of running and breathing, of sensory deprivation, reverses itself and merges, making me feel as if we can run forever. The incandescent glow of the moon distorting and projecting the unworldly shadows of Joshua trees swaying back and forth over this pathway in front of us only magnifies the feeling. I wonder if this is what the late Chemehuevi runner George Laird meant when he quietly spoke of "the secret way of traveling, which is the old way." A runner by the name of *Kaawi?a* (Rat Penis) was the only Chemehuevi known to travel this way; according to Laird, when Rat Penis ran "with his companions, he ran as they did, but when he went alone, he used his secret method. This was possibly a way of teleportation, but of it only this is known for certain: that it enabled him to arrive at his destination with no lapse of time." A group of Chemehuevi runners followed Rat Penis one day to see just how he did this, but his tracks, Laird wrote, "became further and further apart and lighter and lighter on the sand," until they reached the distant village his tracks pointed to. Wrote Laird: "When at length they reached the village at the mouth of the Gila, they inquired 'Did Kaawi?a come here?' 'Yes,' the people answered, 'he arrived on the day that he had left them [the other runners] just as the sun was rising.'"

But any insight into this ancient knowledge of running quickly dissipates when Dick and I are forced to grapple with the realities of struggling over the gnarly spine of the Paiute Mountains into Paiute Canyon. It is tomb-black in the depths of the canyon, the moondust now lost behind the walls of this defile. The footing is too treacherous to even consider running. And my lips are cracked like dry pie crust. The flimsy plastic bladder of my bota bag broke an hour ago, but I'm reluctant to ask Dick for any of his water. The Chemehuevi runners carried their water in the rumen of the desert bighorn, which could be cooked and eaten as a survival ration if need be. That's when the Chemehuevi still sang, according to Laird:

> *My mountain canteen*
> *will go swinging like a pendulum*
> *swing like a pendulum*
> *my mountain canteen*
> *will go bouncing up and down*
> *will go bouncing up and down*

No such luck with my broken bag, which sags flat and helpless at my side, like fresh road kill. And the drier my lips become, the wetter and colder I imagine Paiute Springs will be, 150,000 gallons of water appearing "magically from the sand" each day.

Voices yelp like coyotes in the distance, as Dick and I swat and flail our way out of a jungle of brush toward a roaring fire. We're late—whatever that means in a desert

whose only timepiece is the cyclical rising and setting of the
sun, moon, and stars—and Dick's support crew has been
worried. But we're happy; in fact we're giddy. "Ah yes,"
Dick says, "the running . . . has been interrupted by a small
adventure." And for no reason, we break out laughing. The
taste of adventure ignites our communal merriment, which
we toast late into the evening.

Herman Grey was a Mojave, a *shul-ya* of the Beaver
Clan, when he wrote in *Tales from the Mojave:* "A test of
endurance for men was a trip into southern California, the
whole distance covered at a jogging trot, to trade for abalone shells." Jim Gaston startles us at daybreak the next
morning with a fragment of abalone shell he'd found lying
next to the crumbling rock walls of old Fort Pah-Ute; like
Camp Cady, Fort Pah-Ute was a military outpost strate-
gically positioned along this leg of the Spanish Trail to protect wagon trains of immigrants as they drove their teams
westward along this ancient trade route. And evidence of
that ancient commerce is now sitting right there, gingerly
cupped in the palm of Jim's hand! Who was the runner?
What song did he sing? What vision did he have? What did
he go through to carry that shell more than two hundred
miles before it was dropped in the sands here a millennia
earlier? Was he a Mojave? Or was he a Walapai, or Havasupai? If either of the latter, did he trade red ocher paint from
river's edge in the western Grand Canyon for the shell that
journeyed here from the Pacific? I don't know.

Maybe I'll see farther down this trade route once I start
down my own shadow pathway along the Hopi-Havasupai
Trail a month from now, but for now these are questions
best left to Dick. As among the Chemehuevi, who inherited
their territorial songs from one generation to the next, this
pathway belongs to Dick, and he still has "a Chemehuevi
mile" of sand and rock to go before he reaches the end of it

at the Colorado River. But he's weary. The hundred-odd miles almost smothered him during the night, and now he's on the verge of either physical collapse or of self-discovery—I can't be certain. He needs to run the final leg of his pathway alone to find out for sure.

The Dead Mountains, which the Chemehuevi knew as White Clay Lightning Flash and which the Mojave considered the "highest mountain in the world," is the last range of desert peaks shielding Dick from the end of his pathway at river's edge. By the time he struggles around the northern end of the Dead Mountains, however, he is so physically and emotionally spent that he looks as if he just stumbled out of a funeral; tears are snaking down his salt-caked cheeks, trailing their own pathways. Yet the river is so close now that he can literally feel it pulsating on the horizon, but the pain in his Achilles' tendon feels as if someone has driven an arrow down the back of his heel and left it sticking out of his foot. Worse, the desert pavement has turned into a frying pan, and his bota bags were both sucked dry an hour ago.

It's strange, then, that Dick sees a rare desert tortoise engaged in its own life-and-death struggle for survival. To the Chemehuevi, the *?Aya* is sacred, "its tough-heartedness equated with the will and ability to endure and survive." On this last day it somehow becomes Dick's own spirit-animal, because it charges his painful run with renewed vigor. One footstep, then another, it feels as though he could walk faster, but he keeps running.

The river is getting closer, slowly, only two miles now; the previous one hundred and twenty eight miles rewind in front of him with the precision of Casebier's words: "Paiute Springs, Rock Springs, Marl Springs, the Mojave Sink . . ." They're synaptic images, really; they may be what Carobeth Laird had in mind when she wrote:

"No more moccasined feet tread silently upon the hard-packed trails whispering *tcawa, tcawa, tcawa* . . . that a whole mode of transportation is lost, never to be regained. Even if the remaining native people increased and prospered, their thought has so departed from the old ways, that there would be no eyes to see desert, mountains, and River as they once were seen."

When Dick finally stumbles into the cool embrace of the Colorado River, voices of joy scream out. He doesn't say much, though. In fact, he's so weary he wonders just what it is he's accomplished, if anything. His eyes, streaked with blood-gorged pathways, tell their own story. That on this final, grueling, stifling hot and dusty day, he may have glimpsed, if only for a moment, the desert, mountains, and river as they once were seen by the ancients who ran before him. And I can only hope for as much if I survive my shadow pathway along the Hopi-Havasupai Trail.

II

It's almost Sunday when the three of us enter the east arm of Moqui Trail Canyon on the western edge of the Grand Canyon. We are weary. Our flimsy clothes are tattered. My bare limbs have been repeatedly slashed, leaving jagged, strawberry-red scratches. And for me, the prospect for survival has never seemed more desperate. It has taken me nearly five days to reach this point, retracing the hairline, aboriginal Hopi-Havasupai Trail 174 miles across the searing *Desierto Pintado* and the great Colorado Plateau. And what I'd originally envisioned as an enchanting journey along the prehistoric trade route from Oraibi to Havasupai has been all but obliterated by a labyrinth of historic wagon trails and modern pickup tracks. Worse, unseasonably hot, dry weather dragged me to my knees, almost permanently, the second day out. So the final leg from Moqui Tank to

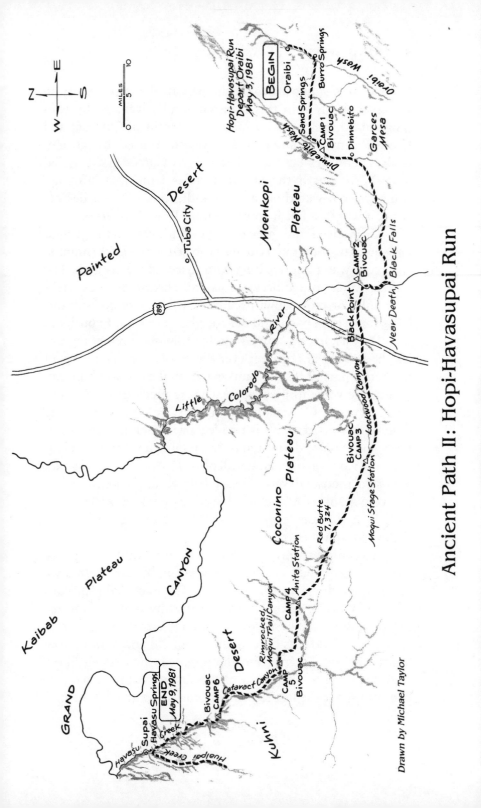

Ancient Path II: Hopi-Havasupai Run

Drawn by Michael Taylor

Havasupai is supposed to be the payoff, the opportunity to step completely into this transtemporal adventure by running wild through the untrammeled depths of Cataract and Havasu canyons, along a pathway first used by ancient traders centuries before Father Francis Garcés first traveled it in 1776. But if the last four miles from that stinking, slime-covered waterhole are any indication of what lies beyond, it will be a finish straight out of Dante's *Inferno*.

Grim-faced, the three of us put our noses to the ground and quickly root out two bathtub-sized *tinajas* brimming with cool water and teeming with insect life. This is the last known water source between us and Havasu Springs, eighteen miles or more downstream. So we "camel up," fill our half-empty bota bags, and debate whether or not to push on.

Dave Ganci has joined me for this life-threatening finish; he is a biped reptile if ever there was one, having spent the better part of his life skulking around the lower Sonoran desert. He votes to bivouac near these precious *tinajas*, but he's carrying an "elephant's foot," a sawed-off sleeping bag that, once stuffed with his two legs, will look like the lower foreleg of a pachyderm. I'm only carrying an "Indian" blanket, so I vote for the balmier depths of Moqui Trail Canyon almost a thousand vertical feet below. Chris Keith is just carrying a Nikon F, and she doesn't care where we bivouac, so long as she gets to photograph the ensuing drama; she is the expedition shooter.

According to my fifteen-minute topographic map, we have two and a half to three miles to run by dark before we can hunker down in the depths of Cataract Canyon, confident that we'll reach Havasu Springs by midmorning tomorrow. But Dave hesitates, explaining that running thirty-four miles in a day is far enough for an old gila monster like himself to run. I agree, but the opportunity to sleep like a dead man in the warm bed of the canyon below is irresistible; I've spent the last four nights curled up around the fire, shivering in my flimsy wool blanket, and I'm as weary and brain dead from those sleepless fire-stokings as I am from the long, hot miles I've run.

I decide to keep moving, but Dave lingers—until I remind him that I'm carrying the food, such as it is: a small bag of wafer-thin piki bread, a few ragged strands of sand-covered beef jerky, and dried apricots, chia seeds, dates, and piñon nuts, also peppered with sand and dirt. He decides to continue.

The three of us scurry along a narrow trail toward 5,660-foot Antelope Point. The trail is really no more than a series of desert bighorn sheep hoofprints mashed into a 45-degree slope, and it's the most exposed and dangerous path any of us has ever been on, far worse than anything I encountered along my inner Canyon pathway the year before. By twilight we still can't find the break through the rimrock indicated on our Supai Quadrangle, so we continue contouring the very edge of the brink, ever mindful of the consequences of a single misplaced footstep. Two to five feet of steep, undeniably loose talus is all that stands between us and the deadly plunge over a relentless wall of Coconino sandstone into the shadowy depths of Moqui Trail Canyon.

By nightfall I know we've been hoodwinked, either by the large, undefinable scale of our fifteen-minute map or by the synergistic combination of sleep deprivation, physical exhaustion, dehydration, and mental fatigue. "Distance running kills brain cells," I tell Chris and Dave, but they are not amused. It is too dangerous to continue or to backtrack, even with Dave's small flashlight, which he now wields as if it's the last source of light on the planet. A haunting precipice looms above us and a gaping abyss yawns below. We can go neither up nor down. We are, as they say of cattle stranded in Utah's canyon country, "rimrocked"—only we are rimrocked on the very edge of northern Arizona's 6,000-foot Coconino Plateau, a land as unforgivingly wild and sublime as it was when anthropologist Frank H. Cushing followed Garcés's century-old trail from the ancient Hopi village of Oraibi to Havasupai in 1882.

And now I am, finally, about to complete my own *entrada* to that same village, along a pathway I've been tracing along Garcés's and Cushing's route across the merciless Painted Desert and stark Coconino Plateau. But where Garcés and Cushing rode horseback along this trade route, guided by the Hopi and Havasupai, I run, as I've theorized ancient traders did before Spaniards introduced horses to this primeval land, running as the Mojaves did along their own leg of the trade route seven suns to the west. But the only guides I have to keep me oriented on this pathway, which bears little resemblance to the Mojave Indian Trail, are the vague personal accounts of Garcés and Cushing, and several scientific papers that attempted to line out the route from one geographical feature, or waterhole, to the next. Unfortunately, Casebier had not yet retraced this regionwide trade route eastward beyond Kingman, Arizona, after linking the historic Beale's Wagon road to it from the east end of the Mojave Indian Trail. Standing there, scratching my head for answers on the edge of that growling black precipice, I long for the same methodical guidance Casebier had provided Dick only a month earlier.

Wherever we are, our only real option is to bivouac where we stand. But there is nothing to anchor our bodies to this mushy powder of cryptogamic soil. Like giant ground sloths, which roamed the western Grand Canyon during the last Ice Age, we carefully paw our way through the dark on all fours down a short, steep sandstone chute toward camp. Camp is a sloping, park-bench-sized ledge covered with dirt, loose rocks, and, no doubt, scorpions; fortunately, it is too dark to see for sure. Standing there, hanging onto the base of a dagger-and-fishhook-covered century plant, we begin sweeping the rock shelf clear of debris with our scuttling feet. A noisy avalanche of stony rubble cascades into the chasm below, covering our faces with swirling dust.

It is cold. The wind is whipping sand into our eyes and ears, but Dave and I cannot control our sudden laughter; it is the nervous laughter of the condemned. Meanwhile, Chris wonders aloud why she actually thanked Tim and me for allowing her to photograph this last perilous marathon.

The laughter abruptly stops when the three of us realize we will somehow have to spend the night out here without sliding into the brink or dying of exposure. The temperature at our Anita Station camp the night before had been in the twenties. Even if there were any piñon or juniper to set ablaze with my knife and flint, there is no room for a fire. So we carefully spread out what vaguely passes for my "genuine Indian blanket," sit on it, then pull it over our shoulders like a shawl, while Dave lays his elephant's foot across our legs, but he keeps the lion's share for himself, until I bring out the food bag. "He who has the sharpest tooth has the finest coat," I tell him, mockingly reminding him of his own wolf-pack philosophy. And so the bartering of food and shelter begins. A trade route, indeed.

Our gnawing hunger temporarily sated with a few precious scraps of food, the three of us spoon our bodies together and reluctantly face the long, dark journey we'll have to make together in order to survive the night. But our airy lair is not the cozy sleeping circle once used by the ancient Serranos of the southern Mojave Desert, who reportedly scraped away the hard desert pavement so that roving tribal members could sleep together for warmth. It is more the smooth divet-indentation of one or two desert bighorn sheep; these animals were once hunted by the Havasupai, who "wore a disguise consisting of a stuffed ewe's head with horns of stuffed buckskin," so that bighorn sheep "might be driven directly over the cliffs." And the next hour or so becomes a restless tug-of-war to make a cold slab of rock more blissful than it ever could be. Since Chris is hunkered down between us, Dave and I toss and turn at her command.

When the scarlet luminescent moments of twilight fade to black, we are greeted by a Milky Way airbrushed across the dark heavens like sparkler smoke, fireballs of shooting stars trailing streamers of fluorescent silver contrails, and tiny white satellites whirling at distant corners of our little piece of the universe, as if they've been fired out of puny earthborne BB guns. For the next eight hours our synaptic reverie will be played and replayed against this celestial cyclorama; tenuously perched as we are, we don't dare close our eyes any more than the Havasupai had, who, according to ethnographer A. F. Whiting, viewed Orion's belt as *amu'u'*, "a flock of bighorn sheep . . . being ambushed by the star Rigel, who was known as Wolf Man (*hatakwila*)."

By midnight the biting cold has penetrated deep within our bones, like the fangs of *hatakwila* himself, and we're on the verge of fibrillating off the edge of our slippery perch. My whimpers are echoed by Chris's and Dave's clacking teeth. Desperately, we reach out for better handholds. Mine is the slick, waxy base of another dagger-tipped century plant, its withered roots loosely anchored to a shallow crack. Chris's is the strap of my bota bag, now choking my shoulder and neck like a lariat. Dave's is his bony right hip smeared onto the rock like the carbon-rubber toe of a climber's boot. Thus set, the three of us resume our private journeys through the night, back along the Hopi-Havasupai Trail.

Oraibi is perched atop a windswept mesa eighty miles east of the Grand Canyon, in the heart of the Painted Desert. Now a secluded, modern Hopi settlement, Oraibi was known by Garcés as Moqui, and it still has the distinction of being the oldest continuously inhabited village in the contiguous United States. Many of its inhabitants steadfastly cling to their ancestral values, although a growing number of Hopi now drive pickups where their grandfathers once ran and rode horses.

Nonetheless, I wasn't sure what they'd think of a *bahanna* (non-Indian) running along an ancient path that once linked their village with that of the Havasupai. In fact, several weeks prior to my departure date, I had sought out the sage advice of Don Decker, a Native American college counselor, because I was troubled by the thought that the Hopi might somehow associate what I was doing with what the controversial Smoki Dancers, a group of white Prescott businessmen, do. The Hopi have long been upset with the Smoki Dancers for performing, for money, sacred Hopi dances inextricably linked to Hopi religion, culture, and lifeways. On the contrary, I had no interest in visiting or photographing the Hopis' sacred trail shrines or in emulating any kind of sacred rites. I was only interested in the trade route from a historic geographer's perspective and in what ancient man—be he Mojave, Havasupai, Hopi, Zuni or whoever—might have endured physically and mentally to cross it. Religion, sacred rites, and ceremony, I felt, were the Hopis' sacrosanct domain. Period.

Decker lowered his glasses, looked me in the eye, and said, "John, if you ask enough people up there, someone will say no. Just go do it."

So that's what I do; I slip out of a small campground adjacent to Oraibi at 4:30 A.M. under the cover of darkness and run through the black sand of Oraibi Wash ten miles south to Burro Springs.

I haven't run two hours west of Burro Springs, however, before I realize that my rim-bound pathway to Supai isn't going to be the wild, near-pristine journey my inner Canyon pathway had been. A series of dirt roads, wagon paths, and horse trails thread the Painted Desert like an indecipherable system of capillaries, a far cry from the "well-beaten trail into the Desierto Pintado" Cushing had followed west from Oraibi a hundred years earlier. It is along the high-speed corridor of this sandblasted maze that the twentieth century comes hurtling back through my aerobic time warp. A young Navajo, driving a beefed-up gun-metal gray Dodge Charger as if he is attempting a land speed record, slides into a red hurricane of his own dust and stops to ask where I'm going.

"Grand Canyon," I yell over the rumbling engine without breaking stride.

"Want a ride," he says, apparently thinking I'm too stoic to stick out my thumb and hitchhike.

"Thanks, no," I tell him. "I'm running to the Grand Canyon," as if that were still the most practical way to reach it.

The Navajo shakes his head, throttles the engine until it shakes and rumbles, and punches it; spitting up fifteen-foot rooster tails of red sand in his wake, he careens down the ancient path, plunging deeper into his own cross-cultural adventure.

By the time I stride into Sand Springs at the thirty-mile mark another hour or so west, I'm wondering if this reaction will be the norm. Three kids and a hairless mutt come running out of a nearby hogan and stand at the side of the sandy track. Their mouths agape, they point at the apparition running toward them and laugh. The dog barks, and suddenly I'm mumbling to myself, "You can run, but you can't hide."

Once a key geographical feature for early travelers in what appears to be an otherwise featureless landscape, Dinnebito (Navajo for People Spring) Wash now forms the northwest border of the 631,194-acre Hopi Reservation. It's late afternoon when I finally rendezvous there with Tim and Craig, eight miles south of Sand Springs. The driving force behind my inner Canyon pathway the year before, Tim and Craig have joined me on this shadow pathway to pursue a similar end: to help this largely ignorant modern man survive an ancient rite of passage, a journey that was commonplace for those who knew the nuances of this austere land and the mode of travel, and for whom primitive survival was second nature. And when Tim and Craig greet me, Chris's motor-drive whining in the background, they make me feel as though I've achieved my first victory in trying to undergo this primeval metamorphosis.

Our camp that first night is a curious mingling of the old and the new. I build my fire with flint and steel; they build theirs with matches and newspapers bearing the headline "Runner Will Relive History in Trip Along Canyon Route." They eat thick bean burros, chased down with cold beer, and sleep in pillowy down sleeping bags. I long to do the same, but I'm trying to see whether I can cross the threshold between the present and the past; so I munch on Native fare of jerky and piñon nuts, and curl around my fire in a brilliant Mexican blanket I'm substituting for an exorbitantly priced genuine Indian blanket. The dichotomy between our two camps is strange though, and I find that I don't want to repeat it again.

Shivering all night around a small fire to the peaceful snoring of Tim, Craig, and Chris, I know by the time first light finally struggles across the eastern horizon that I won't be able to journey back through this aerobic time warp if I'm continually forced to confront the old and the new simultaneously. It's then I realize that I'll have to burn my bridges with Tim and Craig if I'm to experience the same hardships and objective hazards the ancient traders encountered. Without those elements, the pathway would lose its

meaning and authenticity for me. Tim and Craig give me
such selfless emotional and logistical support, I know
they're intent on doing whatever it takes to make my journey a safe one. But I need to at least run from waterhole to
waterhole, as the ancient peoples had, I tell them. They
point out that the day is unseasonably hot and that ancient
peoples generally ran in company of one another, or from
cache to cache or village to village. Today, however, there
are none. So we strike a compromise; we'll rendezvous at
Black Falls on the Little Colorado River at high noon.

By 8 A.M. I realize I've burned all my bridges. The few
springs and stock tanks I run by are bone dry; I'd counted
on them, as the ancients had, to help me reach Black Falls at
the sixty-eight-mile mark. The two liters of water in my
bota bag won't be enough. It's the driest I've seen northern
Arizona in years; worse, the thermometer is pushing ninety
degrees in the shade. And my mind and body begin feeling
as if they're undergoing a primeval metamorphosis like that
experienced by Eddie Jessup, the Harvard professor in *Al-
tered States* who believes "reality can be externalized . . .
[and] remembers himself as primitive man."

For a moment, I falter and my running feels less graceful. I can feel the moisture being sucked out of my body and
lungs with each footfall. And for the first time in sixty miles,
I have doubts about my ability to reach the Little Colorado
River alive. It's too hot. Without extra water, my brain will
boil like cauliflower and I'll drop in my tracks. I've got to
slow down and walk; it's the only way to get the most out of
what little fluid may be left in my body. But walking takes
too much time. I'm having trouble enough trying to run
through this cerebral wildland; walking it would be unbearable. So I continue running, knowing I am treading the fine
line between simple heat cramps and terminal heat exhaustion. Of the same desert, Cushing wrote: "Only the beaten
trail before us, the bones, sometimes human, the bits of

castaway cordage, show that man has ever penetrated its solitudes. Tortured by thirst . . . "

Shimmering in the distance is the blue outline of Black Point. To the south of this massive hump a cresting wave of lava flows, cinder cones, and dormant volcanoes ripple south toward the base of the 12,633-foot San Francisco Mountains. To people like the Hopi, Navajo, Yavapai, and Walapai, these mountains are sacred, the dwelling place of deities. To the Navajo, "these mountains are our father and mother. We come from them; we depend on them . . . each mountain is a person. The water courses are their veins and arteries. The water in them is to their life as our blood is to our bodies." And as I run toward them through a stifling wall of heat, I now view these snowcapped peaks with my own reverence; for a moment, maybe an hour, they seem to draw me toward their center, and I feel as though I'm being whisked back through time.

It wasn't far from here that Garcés stopped at a *ranchería* of thirty Yavapais and wrote: "There arrived later two Indians from Moqui, dressed in leather jackets . . . and they came to trade with these Yavapais, and the word was sent to a neighboring *ranchería*." Running in the footsteps of these ancient traders, I am alone out here, as alone as anyone could ever hope or want to be in our global village, and that fills me with contentment; while the terrain isn't nearly as dramatic as my inner Canyon pathway—or perhaps because of it—I've achieved a sense of isolation and vulnerability when the land, the elements, the endless running begin to strip away societal roles and costumes, when I no longer examine my past or present motives, when my ego feels as though its been hammered into a malleable piece of scrap iron, when I am simply motion.

My feet pad softly across the sandy desert floor. Mushrooms of red sand erupt beneath each footfall. My arms flap in stark rhythm to the ghost-beat of a sun-bleached hawk skeleton lying by the side of the track. I suck hot air through cracked lips. There is no pain, no effort. The only feeling I have is that of dry tumbleweed being blown across the red sand for as far as I can see.

Heat waves shimmer on the western horizon below Black Point, like a curtain of dirty lace that filters out all perceptible color. It's as if the only colors that exist out there in the smog- and haze-shrouded distance are a gray and grayer—if you can call them colors. Yet through this diffused, somber light I see a man on horseback. Is it Dehydration, my own Fifth Horseman of Apocalypse, or merely a Navajo sheepherder? I'm not sure. My arms and legs are no longer glistening with sweat, a telltale sign that without water, death is imminent. My perception seems stultified, and I wonder if I've already begun an irreversible slide toward heat exhaustion, audio distortion, visual hallucinations, death.

I continue running but not consciously. I feel more like the wax figure of a runner, and that my movement is triggered by the most atavistic of instincts: to get to water and to survive. Even if I could sit down and wait for my Road Warrior friend to come screaming over the horizon to my rescue, I wouldn't make it. There is no shade out here in the middle of this godforsaken waste, no water, no aid station, no crowd cheering me on. Nothing. Worse, the only finish line is some nebulous point on the distant horizon five suns west of here. Yet my body keeps racing the sun toward that fleeing horseman. Is he real? Or have I already reached that point when I'll soon get down on all fours and start lapping up the hot sand and gravel as if it were snowmelt tumbling down off the San Francisco Mountains?

The deadly treadmill I'm locked onto, and the buttes, mesas, sand dunes now smothering it, is also sacred land to the Hopi, as Hopi elder Thamas Benyacya was quoted as saying:

"It was given to the Hopi people the task to guard this land, not by force of arms, not by killing, not by confiscation of properties of others, but by humble prayers, by obedience to our traditions and religious instructions, and by being faithful to our creator, Masau'u."

. . . and I wonder if the Fifth Horseman I'm racing toward isn't a solar hologram, a prismic projection of the horseback Hopi we met the day before I left Oraibi. "Going the Hopi way to Supai?" he asked. Yes, we told him. "Lo-o-n-n-ng way," he said. By the time *Lo-o-n-n-ng way, Lo-o-n-n-ng way* is resonating through my bones like a Native American chant, I'm beginning to wonder if the Hopi don't have their own version of the *cuukutiiravi*, the Chemehuevi mile, to strand outsiders like myself a day short of the next waterhole.

My support crew hears its own strange voices when I finally reach Black Falls in the white heat of noon. "As you came around the bend," Craig later said, "we heard this gasping—a death chant. You stumbled over the water and fell in." I remember collapsing face down in the water, my overheated body hitting the water with a nearly perceptible hiss. I remember lying there a lo-o-n-n-ng time, trying to cool my overheated inner core, wondering what happened to the horseman, wondering if ancient runners suffered the same way, or if they all used the "secret way of traveling . . . which is the old way" that Carobeth Laird wrote of. How else did they run a hundred miles a day, day in and day out? I didn't have a clue. I was only trying to run forty.

By the afternoon of Day 3, I think I've accidentally discovered what the "old way" is: to dissociate from the physical act of running, so that my mind can float from one geographical feature to the next. Fortunately, my pituitary gland is releasing enough dreamy endorphins to delude me into thinking I'm running the thirty-eight miles from Black Falls to Moqui Stage Station atop the Coconino Plateau in the tracks of *Kaaw?a* himself. Throughout the day and others to come the running takes on a certain mystical quality. It's as if I have unknowingly made a spiritual rite of passage by coming so close to death. Not that giant fluorescent-green geckos are running with me, or that three-headed chuckwallas are dancing in the flames of every century plant I run past; it's just that an unspoken, unseen energy starts gelling between me and my support crew, between us and the land, as we travel independently of one another across the Coconino Plateau. There isn't any other explanation we could come up with for reaching each rendezvous point almost simultaneously.

Because I know I have to maintain a right-brained grasp of physical reality in order to know which spur road to take, I learn to approach each of these interminably long days of running as if I were going to work, dutifully punching my time card into sunrise and sunset. But there are always too many roads spiraling off in too many directions, and too many miles, and it becomes difficult not to dissociate from the physical act of running, the dreary midday scenery, and pass the day running through my mind. And when I relapse into that inner world, time, space, and geography serve only as a backdrop to my running. Yet somehow, out in the middle of that parched landscape, we meet: Tim, Craig, Chris, me. Dead on! And Craig says, "We just got here. How'd you get here so fast?" "The old way," I say. We shake our heads and laugh, wondering if we really don't have our own ally to guide us down this ancient path.

None of us can forget the man we'd met in Flagstaff the week before, who told us he "taught the old way to young kids." He seemed to know what we were up to. We were in the parking lot of a large shopping center, and we'd just finished loading our supplies into Craig's pickup when the short Hopi man quietly approached us. He was good-looking, healthy, probably in his early sixties, with a slight

paunch, and he was visibly amused that we were busy duct-
taping a plastic tarp over the bed of the pickup. "Maybe it'll
keep the rain off," he said. Tim tapped on it with the palm
of his hand and said, "This is our drum." The old fellow
laughed, tapped on it himself, then started dancing in place,
as if in step to a chantway. We all laughed. "Should work,"
he said, still laughing at the white man's four-wheel-drive
tom-tom. "I'll have to try that." And then, without any
forewarning, he walked away, silently, expressionless, as if
he hadn't seen us. "Hey, Good-bye . . . bye . . . ," we yelled,
trying to get his attention. Suddenly, he wheeled in his
tracks, stared at us with the pleasant, calm demeanor of the
knowing, and said, "See you in dreamland." We stood there
dumbfounded. And here we are five days later, three of us
perched on the very rim of northern Arizona, while Tim
and Craig beat cheeks down the Hualapai Canyon cutoff to
Havasu Springs for a jubilant rendezvous we might not
make for at least another day, if we make it at all. We are as
isolated and vulnerable to death as anyone on earth. Yet,
watching my reveries dance across this cosmic veil, I realize
we are as close to "dreamland" as we can ever hope or want
to be.

It's time; the three of us know it. There is no postpon-
ing it. Daylight will soon be upon us. The sun is already
burning across the Coconino Plateau, and it is about to turn
everything in its path to dust, shoe leather, or corpses.
Slowly, we unlock our human pretzel. Our bones creak like
wooden boards; muscles groan like rusted machinery; our
brains feel like soggy oatmeal.

Dave and Chris have been running with me only a day
and already their eyes bear the mark of the land, of their
private inner journeys. Framed in a mop of curly, shoulder-
length brown ringlets, Chris's face is gaunt; her eyes have

lost their luster, and she is cold and nervous. Dave's hair sticks up in the air like unruly clusters of porcupine quills; his face is flushed, his eyes are almost swollen shut, and his mustache has been tugged down into a worried Fu Manchu. I'm not sure what I look like, but after five days and nights of running and sleeping in the dirt, I feel as if I no longer have any connection whatsoever with the twentieth century.

What I do know is that somehow we're still alive, that together we've survived the night. But the prevailing mood is that we've been condemned to serve out a life sentence of running through a canyon gulag, and that we're about to enter terminal confinement unless we can miraculously find a way to escape.

"Boy that was fun. . . . I wouldn't have missed that for anything." Snippets of dialogue swirl around the three of us as we claw our way along the deadly rim of Moqui Trail Canyon in an attempt to locate its namesake path into the depths. The canyon now roars with color in the early morning light. When Cushing reached this point a century earlier, his words described our own struggle to reach the floor of Cataract Canyon alive:

> Who would have imagined that between the terraced plains which we saw ahead and the one we were passing through was a canyon, which, though narrow, was so deep that no one could cross it for miles up or down its length? Even the entrance to that tremendous chasm can scarcely be pictured . . . [a] descent of twelve-hundred feet, almost vertical, except to say that we here wound around a great bank of talus, with tons upon tons of rock impending above us, there scrambled over great rocks, and crept along a foot-wide trail, where one misstep would have precipitated us hundreds of feet.

Even without Cushing's forewarning, it is going to be one of those days—I know. After five hours of terror-fraught backtracking, and another stifling hour of debating the merits of Dave's suggestion that we head thirty miles back to Grand Canyon Village for water instead of fifteen miles to Havasu Springs, we finally reach Jwa Qwaw Gwa Spring on the floor of the Moqui Trail Canyon. We are out of food. Jwa Qwaw Gwa Spring (Bachathaiva) is dry. And just to drive home the point, some clever Havasupai has hung the sun-bleached skull and horns of a steer above the water tank as an omen of what lies behind.

After sniffing and pawing around the dry waterhole like a couple of mangy lobos, we find what looks like six bags of horse feed. "At least we'll have oats," Dave says. "Open it," I tell him. Peering through the 35mm lens of her Nikon, Chris frames the scene of two grown men about to pillage what they think is a Havasupai food cache. But she breaks out laughing when she sees powdered cement pouring out of the slit in the top bag. "The final fuck you," Dave says, staring at six ninety-pound bags of *Ready Mix*. And there's not a drop of water in sight. I lick the imaginary granola from my lips, and the three of us start back down Moqui Trail Canyon.

When Cushing traveled down Cataract Canyon to Havasupai in 1882, he counted "forty-three abrupt turns . . . each one deeper, each turn narrowing the vision . . . [until] only a narrow strip of sky could be seen from our pathway." Cushing had counted and knotted those turns on the fringe of his buckskin shirt. By the time I knot nine turns on a string dangling from my blanket, the immense walls of Cataract Canyon are swaying above me and I realize the day is going to be a rerun of Black Falls.

The heat is appalling. We are dangerously low on water at two quarts each, and we have entered what Cushing called the Kuhni Desert, a stranglehold of impenetrable sandstone walls, dry sand, and brittle foliage. There will be no four-wheel-drive pickups waiting for us around the next bend, only horseback Havasupai cowboys savvy enough to venture into this heat. But the only horses we see are skinny, paranoid nags that look as if they've been strung out on fluid deprivation for so long that they don't know whether they're up canyon or down. They're pale, ashen apparitions of the bleached skeletons that litter the floor of the canyon, as if they've been gassed by some deadly toxin.

Jwa Qwaw Gwa Spring failed us without mercy; somehow, we have to make it to Havasu Springs on the water we have left. I wonder if we won't suffer the same fate as these ponies, swaying back and forth on knees that are about to buckle any moment, this canyon desert ready to snuff out yet three more lives. Walls erupt out of the barren floor of this canyon for hundreds of feet, hemming us in a hell that offers two ways out: death or Havasu Springs, whichever comes first. So running these last few miles is no longer a relevant concern. The only thing that carries any weight is survival, and if surviving means having to walk the last few "Indian miles" into Havasu Springs, so be it. I couldn't survive another hot, dry run like Black Falls; my body is too run-down and I'm now responsible for the lives of two of my mates.

But even walking, I don't think survival's really in the cards unless we can find water somewhere along the way. The prickly pear cactus and other succulents we'd normally rely on in such a perilous situation are so dry and withered they look as if they've been freeze-dried into the powdery red earth. If worse comes to worst, I tell myself, we can always corner one of those horses and stone it to death. I try this thought out on Dave and he agrees; if that's what it takes, bring out the war clubs. Chris is understandably shocked by such talk, but we are rapidly approaching the point of being reduced to cave dwellers—if we haven't already stepped over that line. "Come on," I sing out, in a pathetic attempt to humor my companions, "it's right around the next bend." And the next. And the next. Down this twisting defile the three of us trudge on toward certain oblivion.

I drift back, out of this canyon, not to ancient traders journeying in and out of it, but to a year ago, near the end of my inner Canyon pathway, when Tim told me, "John, you can't run to Supai." I'd thought about that the entire year I trained for this pathway in the mountains surrounding Prescott, the repeated long-distance phone calls I'd placed to Supai tribal headquarters in hopes of speaking with the tribal chairman himself to get permission to cross the Traditional Use Area. But I never got past the secretary. She always gave me the same answer: "He's not in. You have to hike down from Hualipai Hilltop and get a permit." The Havasupai were justifiably big on hiking and camping permits, because the revenue they generated formed the backbone of their economy. But I wasn't a hiker, and I had no intention of going near any sacred shrines. I only wanted to run in the footsteps of ancient traders, and if they crossed those of Sinyella, then it was said:

> When I was six years old, my father said, "Do not sleep after sunrise; wake as soon as daylight appears. Run toward dawn. You should do this every day. Run out as far as you can. Do not walk, run. Do this always when you are a young man too; then you will be able to run fast, and when you race someone you will win. If you do not, you will be beaten.

As the Havasupai receptionist had done to me over the phone, without running. She had no idea what I was talking about when I tried to explain I was running from Oraibi to Supai. Trade route, what's that? So I decided that when, and if, I reached Moqui Trail Canyon the second time around, I would follow Don Decker's advice to "Just go do it, John."

If shivering around a bivouac fire every night, gnawing on piñon nuts and jerked meat, and running more than two hundred miles along the ancient route of commerce into Supai wasn't "traditional use" of the area, what was? If the

Havasupai—much more probably the B.I.A.—wanted to arrest me for spiritually linking my pathway from Oraibi to Supai, it no longer mattered. Strap on the leg irons, cover my face with a black hood, and parade me through the village. Where better to spend my first night in jail than in the center of the earth, eating Havasupai peaches and frybread, and watching nubile boat "hags" (their term) trek up from the Colorado River to watch the hanging?

"Where's Dave?" Chris yells, and suddenly I'm jerked back into the physical reality of this dream track.

"I don't know," I yell back, now wondering what on earth my eyes have been focusing on. "Check for footprints," I say.

We zigzag back and forth along the main stem of Cataract Canyon, wearily dragging our feet in the sand until we find Dave squatting on all fours, digging for water with both hands. "What's it look like?" I ask him.

"Dry, the whole place is dry." The three of us look at each other, now fearing that we'll be sharing a common grave. "The final fuck you," Dave says.

We turn and plod back toward impending doom, wondering how much closer to death we'll have to trudge before we're forced to slit the throats of one of these scrawny horses and drink their blood. But this isn't the Mojave Desert and we're not Kit Carson, any more than this is the Galiuros and we're trapping beavers with mountain man James Ohio Pattie. This is the twentieth century, and people in America no longer kill horses and antelope to drink their blood and survive. So Dave and I make a pact to try to hold out a little longer; these horses have to be getting water somewhere, we figure. Chris, however, has since resolved to accept her fate, now revering these horses no less than the Hindu reveres the sacred cow.

We pull out all the stops that afternoon in our desper-

ate search for water, but the maidenhair ferns, a sure indicator of perennial and intermittent springs, are as brown and
brittle as straw. Even the trickling seeps we'd counted on
finding in the horizontal cracks and fissures of Supai sandstone are dry. There's no way out, and we have no other
options, death or Havasu Springs, whichever comes first.

When twilight finally seeps into the canyon like a cool,
dark rivulet of water, a chorus of crickets echoes through
this defile like the willowy legs of ancient split-twig figur-
ines dancing across old deer hide. Then comes darkness,
and mindless chatter about where we are. It doesn't matter.
We stop. We're not sure where, only that we're downstream
from where we were last night. I gather tinder and ignite a
brilliant yellow flame with the first strike of my flint, while
Dave and Chris shuffle around in the semidarkness gathering firewood. Even without a handheld mirror, our
wretched physical images reflect those of the living saw-
horses peering at us from across the wash. They obviously
haven't found water either. "You can lead a runner to water,
but you can't make him drink it," I say, giddy from fatigue
and dehydration. Nobody pays any attention.

In *Prehistoric Trade in the Southwest,* Harold S. Colton
wrote:

> Over this thousand miles of trail, shell from the [Pacific]
> coast passed to points on the [Coconino] plateau and along
> the route other objects passed east and west. . . . The Wala-
> pai Indians killed deer or mountain sheep and traded the
> hides to the Havasupai, for woven goods procured from the
> Hopi. The Havasupai in their homes tanned the hide and
> traded it to the Hopi for woven goods and pottery. The Hopi
> manufactured the buckskin into white boots for their
> women or traded the hides or boots to the Zuni or Rio
> Grande pueblos, receiving in return turquoise from Santo
> Domingo, Mexican indigo from Isleta and buffalo skins
> from the plains.

We, too, are traders, and we haggle and barter around the fire that night for our own precious commodities. Dave offers a cup of his water, which he carried from Moqui Tank, for eight of my jojoba beans. I count them out on my blanket: one, two, three, four, five, six, seven, eight! But my beans have traveled further, more than two hundred miles north from the McDowell Mountains, ancestral lands of the ancient Salado People and the Hohokam culture. To me they are more precious than cashews, and I demand two cups. He hesitates; Chris smiles. "Throw in four aspirin, and you've got a deal." Agreed.

With the crude strokes of Cro-Magnon man, Dave mashes these beans with a makeshift mortar and pestle, and sets his metal cup in the coals of our fire to brew up a hot cup of waxy, bitter jojoba bean "coffee." I give Chris half a cup of my water, before using the other half to chase down the bitter white powder of a three-course aspirin dinner. "I'm saving the other cup for morning," I warn them both, "so don't get any ideas." I curl around the fire and try sleeping with one eye open, while Chris frames the scene, and Dave explores yet another version of his oft-repeated "days of wooden ships and iron men" theme.

We wake long before dawn the following morning and breakfast on the continental servings of two aspirin "over easy," a baby-pee-warm mug of water each, and a side of dust. It is a light breakfast, for sure, but we start loping toward dawn with renewed vigor, red dust whooshing up and down our bare legs with each footfall. We are trying desperately to go fast, now, in hopes of beating the merciless sun into the pit of Cataract Canyon. But the miles peel off slowly, with the writhing tedium of a Mojave rattlesnake molting its scaly, parchment-thin skin. And as we journey into one turn and around and out through the next, we soon return to the mindless trance of the day before. And I drift back again, out of this endless gorge, to Day 4 of this pathway, and I wonder if today could possibly be any worse.

Day 3 had almost been my nemesis on the inner Canyon pathway the year before. And Day 4 along this rim-top shadow pathway was no different: not long after rolling up my blanket and dousing the fire—spiritually, physically, and mentally—I did not want to be running across the Coconino Plateau. The whole idea of running—anywhere, for any reason—repulsed me. "Why would anybody want to do that?" I asked myself point-blank.

But there were others following this pathway, and I would not let them down, so long as I could take another step. Tim Ganey, for one, was the expedition point man. For Tim, "the adventure began in that crowded Safeway parking lot . . . when that Hopi came up and greeted us as if he knew what we were up to. All your life you could have waited for him, but it could have happened only on that one day, because the chemistry was right." Craig Hudson was another, Tim's counterweight and the most levelheaded among us. At first Craig wondered what on earth he "was doing out there in the middle of the Painted Desert, other than it would develop into an adventure . . . [but] I soon realized I was getting ripped out of society and stuck in a magical place." Christine Keith was the third, the tireless photojournalist who ran every step of that impossibly grueling thirty miles from Moqui Stage Station to Anita Station on Day 4. While Tim and Craig shadowed us, she was the one who picked me up every time I sat down to quit, prodding me on as I sobbed and whimpered: "Come on, Annerino! Not much further." My ankle had felt then like a coyote's forepaw caught in a bloody steel trap; I only wondered whether I was going to have to chew it off to escape the excruciating pain every time my left foot kissed the earth. I couldn't let them down, any more than I could let

Dave down. On less than thirty miles of training a week, he had run forty-one miles with me on Day 5. Physically and emotionally it had been my best day, because I woke up feeling as though I was born into this world to do nothing but run wild along this pathway—the two of us chewing up the piñon-studded Coconino Plateau to Moqui Tank because our "legs were like horses."

These friends and soulmates were reason enough to continue yesterday and the day before that. But how would it end now? I wasn't sure; it could go either way. I only knew I should have done Cataract Canyon alone. It was too stark and desperate a place this year to bring anyone else along. But Tim and Craig had thought it wise for me to be accompanied through Cataract's Brobdingnagian depths, and Chris and Dave had wanted to share in the excitement of the "summit push." I didn't argue with any of them. Even after a year of difficult training, I knew this impossible pathway was far beyond my grasp without them, and I trusted their judgment implicitly. I only wondered if after suffering with me, Dave and Chris would find the same significance in the lost oasis of Havasu Springs that I did; or, if we actually reached it alive, would they remember it as a nightmare, as I feared Margie had the year before?

Before I can answer my own cross-examination, though, I stop dead in my tracks. I'm staring a Havasupai right in the eyes. He's not a mirage, a hologram, or even a hallucination—at least I don't think he is. He's sitting on a short, healthy-looking roan and he's the epitome of contentment, a man who's discovered the very essence of life. A large, round belly hangs over his hands, which are clasped around a rope-worn saddlehorn; his tan cheeks puff out jowllike, and a glint stirs in his eyes like little penlights.

"Where'd you come from?" he says. But he already knows. The echo of strangers travels far and fast, as it always has, in this timeless land.

"Oraibi, six days ago," I say proudly, as if we've both transcended time and it's still the perfectly natural thing to do. He stares down at me; I'm dressed up, except for my shoes, in what I imagine might vaguely pass for an ancient Native American runner's clothing. I stare back at him; he is dressed in what he thinks a cowboy might once have worn. A bond has been forged; we both continue to stare at one another, smiling. And I wonder if this is the lesson I'm to learn from this pathway, that each of us has tried to explore each other's past in order to go forward? Or perhaps it's that survival isn't something you learn once, but something you should live with as closely as your own heartbeat, as the ancient Native American traders had, the ones who traveled to Supai and *back* from the Mojave Indian Trail seven suns west of here, and from the Moqui villages three suns east. I'm not sure. Maybe the lesson I've learned can't be verbalized; it may be the unknowing, the unspoken. Then again it may be nothing, nothing at all.

I mumble something to him about having to push on. I don't know what else to say, but nothing else really needs to be said. He's found enlightenment on horseback; I've found exhaustion, at least for the moment, on foot.

He turns and resumes riding up Cataract Canyon, through his own dreamscape. I turn and start for Havasu Springs, wondering why I hadn't asked him for a long pull from his felt-covered gallon canteen? Was I trying to prove I could be as stoic as any Native American runner? I no longer have a clue. I only know Chris and Dave are somewhere behind me, I am not exactly sure where. But we've made it, because as I come around that "forty-third abrupt turn" once knotted in Cushing's buckskin fringe, I find aluminum cans strewn about the sandy floor of the canyon. It's a sure indicator that civilization is not far off, because anyone who carries soda instead of a canteen into the Kuhni Desert does not stray far from creature comforts. All I have to do is run another mile into Havasu Springs to the end of this pathway, and it will all be over—at least for another year. And only time will tell whether Tim, Craig, and I will hear the silent siren call to venture into the unknown together again.

I turn, wait for the shadows of Dave and Chris floating in the distance, then press on toward the infinity of the moment, running as I never have before. Running wild.

CHAPTER SIX

Savage Arena

*As the departure date grew
nearer, the full consequences
of going . . . to the Himalaya made
their impact. I seriously doubted
if I was going to come back.*

Peter Boardman
The Shining Mountain

It is dawn. A nerve-jangling wind is howling through the ponderosas, and a late winter storm threatens to engulf northern Arizona's eight thousand–foot Kaibab Plateau. I am shivering, not only from the cold that cuts me to the bone, but also from the fear that rattles my core. I am standing on the eastern escarpment of this densely wooded plateau, staring down the dark throat of Nankoweap Canyon, and I am about to unleash myself on the most dangerous pathway I've ever faced. I haven't been marched to this brink at gunpoint; I have come here willingly, again, along a spiritual path as winding and elusive as the physical one I'm about to descend. It is a journey that, if I'm very, very lucky, will finally prove, at least to me, that ancient traders could have run through this glorious chasm centuries before the first horseback Europeans ever laid eyes on it. But if I'm not so lucky, if I fail as I assume I will, I hope to get out of this canyon alive.

That's why I've dreaded this moment for an entire

year; the entire year I've trained for just this moment has dogged me with such fear that for the first time in my life I'm seriously questioning the dangerous path I'm about to descend—because it leads through the very jaws of the earth, and even if dinosaurs no longer roam its fearsome depths, my own dragons have repeatedly come back to haunt me since reaching Havasu Springs the year before. I knew all along that the succession of pathways I'd been following pointed in only one direction—the North Rim. Like a climber who's been guided by the hand of fate up the highest mountain in the world by two previous routes, I was inexplicably drawn to attempt this last dangerously elegant line through the Grand Canyon, no matter what logical or theoretical excuses I offered myself or anyone else.

But Tim, Craig, and I had originally thought the South Rim was impossible and the Hopi-Havasupai Trail incomprehensible; the North Rim was truly both. Of the estimated 250-mile-long route that courses east to west through the seldom-explored frontier below the North Rim, fewer than fifty miles follow any kind of trail. I would die trying to run such a precipitous route, whatever my reasons. Bolstered by our two back-to-back successes, and Ginny Taylor's own unwavering voice of confidence, however, Tim and Craig thought overwise. "Look at Messner," another voice told me. But there was no comparing myself to the Himalayan superstar; Reinhold Messner was the first man in history to climb the world's fourteen 8,000-meter peaks without oxygen. And the second time he climbed Everest without oxygen he had climbed it solo! Yet owing to my own image of the man, I at least had a way to gauge the impossible scale of the trackless North Rim; I could envision someone else running it solo, but not me. Yet the further I explored the image of a man confronting the North Rim, the more I took to examining the impossible challenge two Britons had overcome. Joe Tasker and Peter Boardman were inexplicably drawn together to attempt what the world climbing community then knew was impossible: an ascent of the imposing, ice-plastered, mile-high West Wall of 22,520-foot Changabang in India's Garwahl Himalayas. Tasker and Boardman presented their case to the British climbing community in hopes of securing funding to at least reconnoiter the route for a future attempt. "Impossible," they were told. Undeterred, Tasker and Boardman took leaves of absence to go have a look at this impossible wall; in the true spirit of mountaineering, they just wanted to see how far up they could get before storms, avalanches, altitude, or the inhuman scale of the wall forced them to retreat. Once on the West Wall, however, Tasker and Boardman kept climbing, and climbing, until, as Tasker wrote in his diary, "without stopping to talk about it, by some imperceptible transition of thought, it was clear we could climb the West Wall, provided we could stick it out." They did.

Knowing of their remarkable success, I still thought the North Rim was too big, too dangerous, and too remote for me to run. Unlike my inner Canyon pathway and the Hopi-Havasupai Trail, where my resupply crew was able to reach me nearly every day, I would be virtually cut off from all logistical support and emergency help; it was then that I realized the North Rim might be the ultimate pathway—not for me, but for someone else. I just wanted to "go have a look," to see how far I could get before I'd have to turn back. Then, that's why I fear this very moment. I know that once I step off the edge of the planet there would be no turning back, because the Canyon has a way of sucking you into its timeless embrace, however you approach it.

A primal fear surges through me as I start running full bore down the icy Nankoweap Trail. It is here, only moments out, that the world suddenly avalanches beneath my tumbling legs and feet, sliding and cascading through the

Kaibab limestone, the Coconino sandstone, the Redwall limestone, through layer upon layer of geologic history all sandwiched together in rainbow-hued steps, back through 1.2
billion inconceivable years, until my eyes pick out that thin
strand of angel hair called Nankoweap Creek. It is here,
free-falling into the abyss, that I want to turn around—
should turn around—and slam the door on this final pathway before it's too late.

But *it is* too late, and I keep running, endlessly down,
down, down, knowing why I had shuddered with such fear
when I said good-bye to Chris May and Chris Keith only
minutes before—because once I reach the terminus of the
faint Nankoweap Trail, I will be completely cut off from the
rest of the world. Success and survival will rest solely on my
ability to adapt to the extremes of weather, terrain, loneliness, and fatigue. Every move I've made in my life, every
judgment I've ever made, right and wrong, will tip the scales
one way or the other. Out here, there is no room for error.
One seemingly inconsequential mistake, like not tying my
shoes properly, could cause me to slip and fall, and if I get
hurt or knocked unconscious it will be as if I've stepped off
the face of the earth. Below the North Rim, there's little
chance anyone would actually find me alive. And perhaps it
was for that reason more than any other, that just ten days
ago—after an exceedingly difficult year of training—I still
didn't know whether I was going to attempt the North Rim
or not. I was torn. The odds of running the North Rim and
surviving were too frightening to consider.

Much of my unrelenting fear had to do with marginal
access; access from the North Rim for my resupply crew is,
in fact, totally out of the question. Besides the unmaintained
trail I am barreling down, there are only two other practical
routes descending the 350-square-mile North Rim between
here and Thunder River, the end of this proposed pathway:

the North Kaibab Trail, which bisects this pathway near the midway point, and the unmaintained Shinumo Trail three days beyond the Kaibab. But as far as the "keepers of the gates" are concerned, the North Rim is closed until the snow melts. Consequently, all support will have to come from South Rim, which presents a logistical nightmare. No matter how we slice this pie, each scheduled resupply point is a minimum two day's journey apart for me, and two of them necessitate dangerous river crossings in forty-degree water. The magic act will not just be to reach them, but to reach them at the same time that my small support crew does, leapfrogging as they will be from one trail to the next.

There was also the question of emergency evacuation to consider. But after a year of analyzing my escape routes and options, I considered helicopter rescue by the Park Service out of the question. It was my pathway and I would have to personally assume whatever risks were involved in trying to complete it. It wasn't fair to put someone else's life in jeopardy if something went wrong with my plans. Ancient traders didn't have air support. They adapted or died, based on their own judgment and experience. And if I was to learn those same lessons, lessons long buried by modern society, I was going to have to risk running the brink alone. And that made me tremble whenever I thought about the possibility of making a mistake.

Still flying on the wings of fear, as the sun strains to break through the ominous layer of gray clouds hemming in the Desert Facade like a great wall, I have but one thought: I must reach the Colorado River at Lava Canyon tonight. Tim, Craig, and I originally thought I should take two days to attempt this first leg, but I am now so dwarfed by the imposing scale of the North Rim and so caught off guard by the fact that I've actually embarked on a pathway I know is impossible that the only way I can put the rest of this pathway into manageable perspective is to somehow reach the Colorado River tonight. If I can do that, the route will at least make theoretical sense. But I really can't think in terms of reaching Thunder River, which I won't see, if I see it at all, for seven to ten days. It's beyond my comprehension at this point. Nor can I really think of reaching the Colorado River except as the completion of a tentative first step and nothing more. I'm so awed by the North Rim—perhaps because of what I had experienced below the South Rim— that I will have to focus on simply putting together enough footsteps until scenes unreeling from the past dictate the rhythm and mood of this pathway.

Chased by the haunting apparitions of time and distance, I'm forced to stop a half hour out when the trail plummets off into the void. I take a deep breath and stare up at swirling, black clouds spitting pellets of icy snow down on me. There is little time to waste. Another few minutes and my route will be covered with ice. Tentatively, I start across a sloping cinder ledge, kicking the toes of my running shoes into the mushy soil as if they're crampons and using my bare fingers on the cold, brittle rock to keep myself from being sucked into the gaping maw several thousand feet below. I try not to think of the consequences; I can only move tentatively, in the hopes of completing this icy traverse without slipping.

Of the four named trails that slide off the North Rim, the Nankoweap has perhaps the most peculiar history. According to J. Donald Hughes's *The Story of Man at the Grand Canyon*, the Nankoweap Trail was constructed by John Wesley Powell and geologist Charles Doolittle Walcott during the winter of 1882, so that Walcott could study "the Grand Canyon series of rock layers" that he had discovered "were much older than had been thought." How much older? It's beyond my comprehension. The fact that Powell and his men "encamped in snow, often concealed for days in driving frozen mist and whirling snow" so that Walcott could spend the remainder of that brutal winter on the floor of Nankoweap Canyon, completely cut off from the outside world, made far more sense to me than doing it to discover whether a rock was 1 or 10 million years old. But the thing that concerns me most right now is that this hand-forged trail, which Walcott called "perfectly frightful," offers me little more than a route to run along its dangerously exposed and crumbly Supai sandstone walls after I complete the traverse.

Once I do, I take a deep breath and start running again, still twitching with fear . . . until I establish a rhythm of melding footsteps into switchbacks and begin careening down one switchback after another. It's then that I start envisioning Uncle Jim Owens. A onetime cowboy from the Good Night Ranch on the Texas panhandle, Owens was appointed Forest Service warden on the North Rim at the turn of the century. But that was akin to hiring the fox to guard the henhouse, because during his twelve years of "game management," Owens reportedly killed 532 mountain lions! By 1930, however, the official North Rim death toll for predators stood at a staggering "781 lions, 554 bobcats, 4,889 coyotes, and 20 wolves." As a result of such drastic conservation measures, the Kaibab deer population mushroomed completely out of control, from 10,000 to 100,000 according to some estimates. Incredibly, a plan was devised to herd some 5,000 deer down the Nankoweap Trail, across the Butte Fault, where it was supposed they would obediently swim the river and walk single file up the Tanner Trail to the South Rim. What nobody guessed, apparently, was that even with 125 horseback men riding arm in arm and firing 45-caliber pistols in the air, wild, half-starved mule deer would have none of it, especially in a snowstorm. That fact was headlined on page one of the Thursday, December 18, 1924, edition of *The Arizona Republican*:

KAIBAB DEER DRIVE IS CALLED OFF
Snowstorm Ends Plans of McCormick. Motion Picture Men Return to Flagstaff in Blinding Snowstorm: Deer Scatter Wildly.

Even Hollywood had gotten in on the deer drive. Thousands of deer died of starvation.

But before this reel completely unwinds, I've reached the floor of Nankoweap Canyon. And reaching this point is a success, I tell myself, but I am overcome more with trepidation than with happiness. I am on the bottom of the Grand Canyon, yes, six thousand vertical feet and more than a dozen miles below 8,424-foot Saddle Mountain, but any thoughts I have of turning back—and I do—are futile. Even if I were now capable of running nonstop up so steep and precarious a trail, Chris May and Chris Keith won't be there to take me out. At this very moment they are making their own frantic dash back to their vehicle at the edge of Houserock Valley before this late winter storm lays in for good.

I look back up at the snow-covered rim, dwarfed by its "brooding canyon walls," and realize I've severed my one known link with the outside world. Is this what Walcott felt in here during the winter of 1882? No doubt. And like Walcott, I am on my own now. My only way out of the Canyon lies southward along the Butte Fault to Lava Canyon, where I'll have to swim the icy river. How far? In miles, I really don't know. It would only be a guess in this trailless terrain. Time and visual distance are my only mileposts with larger symbolic goals like the Colorado River and the Tanner Trail constantly beating on the periphery of my consciousness. In that light, it's easy to understand why Native

Americans once talked in terms of suns and moons when they traveled, as the Chemehuevi had with their own interpretation of a "mile." As far as reaching the river at Lava Canyon, I estimate the distance at "two sleeps." But I'm still overcome with such fear, I know in my bones I am going to try to make it in one.

I boulder-hop across the mossy-wet stones of Nankoweap Creek, turn south, and start running up the steep, scaly spine of the Butte Fault. According to an unconfirmed National Park Service report dated March 27, 1945, the route I've been following since leaving Saddle Mountain, and that I will try to follow all the way to the foot of the Tanner Trail, is the northern leg of the same Horsethief Trail I followed into the Canyon two years earlier. Of it, onetime Colorado miner Peter D. Berry "claimed that after the [horsethief] gang shot it out with the sheriff, one wounded man reached his place at Grand Canyon. Before he died, he confided that a copper kettle at the foot of the Tanner Trail contained the gold collected for [stolen] horses."

I think about that on and off for the remainder of the morning, as I struggle to the top of one ridge line, then fly down its opposite side, the foamy snorts of tired horses and the creak of dry saddle leather filling my ears, the musty smell of sweat and horseshit permeating the air. And I wonder if riding horseback across the corrugated terrain, driving a band of stolen horses, could possibly be any easier than trying to run it.

By the time I reach Sixtymile Canyon, four parallel canyons south of Nankoweap, however, hunger and fatigue sack me. I peel off my two bota bags and unshoulder my twelve-pound rucksack; from it I remove a warm pile jacket and two foil-wrapped bean burros. But as slowly as I try to eat the morning's rations, I swallow them and pass out where I sit. The tinkling music of Sixtymile Creek soothes me, and for a moment, perhaps an hour, the battle with myself is over. Tucked into the cocoon of my warm jacket, pleasant images whisk me far away from this dangerous journey, images of home, family, and friends.

The clock is ticking, though, and before I'm ready I'm back in the middle of the eastern Grand Canyon, rubbing the trail of saliva off my mouth and chin, the sand and sleep out of my eyes. My legs are stiff. I feel as if I've aged ten years. And what lies beyond is the dog work of trying to run the Butte Fault the rest of the way to the river. I swallow three aspirin and gather the contents of my pack, which lay scattered across the ground as if the pack had fallen off a cliff. I refill my two bota bags, drop in some iodine tablets and set off again, striding on cramped legs up the steep saddle dividing Sixtymile from the East Fork of Carbon Creek. The nap has given me a much-needed respite, but it's also provided the fundamental transition between morning and afternoon. Consequently, I'm able to divide the day psychologically into two "short" runs, rather than one interminably long one.

I am choking back a harsh, throat-burning cough when I finally top out on this unnamed 5,000-foot saddle. My legs are knotted with fatigue, and the storm front that's been haunting me all morning finally hammers me. I continue running anyway. Snow and hail pelt the bare slopes around me as I make an uncontrolled dash for the floor of the East Fork of Carbon Creek. I am breaking my own rule of thumb—Never Run So Fast or Carelessly That you'll Break an Ankle—but reaching the Colorado River tonight is everything to me. And I continue flying out of control, leaping over one rock, then another, flapping my arms like wings, using my heels like the metal edges of skis to glide and break, to slow each skidding landing, until I'm dropping so fast and wildly that I no longer can control the speed and precision of my descent, and I'm rolling. Dust and rocks spew everywhere as I try to count the somersaults before I can dig my heels into the steep cinder slope and stop. When I finally do, I continue to lie there, snow stinging my face and arms. I take a deep breath and wonder how badly I am injured. Miraculously, except for some scratches and bruises, I am all right. So I begin looking for a cave to hole up in and lick my wounds.

I find a truck-sized boulder fifty yards upslope from my landing zone. I crawl inside to shiver and worry away the hour it takes the storm to abate. Fortunately, the hail and snow don't stick for long, but when I crawl away from the overhang I stumble through the semidarkness down the steep talus as though I'm trudging through a foot of snow. Gloom overtakes me, not just because of my wreck, but because 6,394-foot Chuar Butte looming high above me is an oppressive reminder of what miscalculations can mean to life out here. According to the July 16, 1956, issue of *LIFE* magazine,

> . . . a Trans World Airlines Super Constellation with 70 aboard and a United Airlines DC-7 with 58 aboard had taken off from Los Angeles three minutes apart on June 30. Approaching the Painted Desert, where their scheduled routes were known to cross, they collided and plummeted over three miles into the Canyon. After both planes had been unreported for several hours, an aerial searcher found two charred and still smoldering smudges high on buff-colored buttes, less than a mile apart near the eastern end of Grand Canyon National Park.
>
> It was unlikely that all the victims would ever be found.

If reporters were calling two commercial airliners carrying 128 people "smudges" down here, what would they call a lone runner who'd flown out of control? All the more reason to keep running, I tell myself. But when I reach the base of Chuar Lava Hill it is beginning to drizzle. My eyelids are heavy with fatigue, and exhaustion is about to bring me to my knees. It is time to bed down for the night, but I keep stumbling until I find what looks like a suitable overhang somewhere along the sandy floor of the West Fork of Carbon Creek. In the fading light I drop my pack and gather what seems like half a cord of firewood. It's going to be a long, drizzly night. So I drag crooked limbs of dead mesquite toward my lair and begin breaking them up into neat two-foot lengths, finally stacking each piece next to my pack for easy reach.

Unless it's a dire emergency, building a fire in the Grand Canyon is illegal; so I reevaluate the necessity of it. Without a fire, I'll get hypothermia; with a fire, the bivouac will be tolerable provided I keep the flames stoked throughout the night. The choice is obvious, as is the location of the fire. I build it beneath the overhang, on the edge of the creekbed, so that summer flashfloods will scour away all traces of my passing. Otherwise, charcoal from my fire, like charcoal from Anasazi fires, could remain for a thousand years or more.

I drift off to the ghost images of shadows dancing against the Canyon walls. An hour later, however, I'm awakened by the cold draft on my back. I turn over, curl up with my back to the fire, and nod off again. A half hour later, I wake up again, turn back over, and add more fuel to the embers. I check my watch; nine hours till sunup. At this rate, I won't get any sleep. I look at my watch again, and in the flickering light, it tells me of another journey. For numbers it has letters; they spell out MILLIONMILER. Below this cipher is printed J. ANNERINO, and below that the name of a trucking company. Looking through the plastic crystal of this cheap retirement watch, I feel a strong kinship and power. MILLIONMILER represents the distance my father has driven an eighteen-wheel tractor-trailer rig without jack-knifing on some rain-slicked highway, or slamming into a concrete abutment, or succumbing to a thousand other heinous accidents. And as I struggle to stay warm, rain ceaselessly dripping from the roof of the overhang, I know that somewhere out there in the real world thousands of drivers like my father are "fighting the white line," desperately trying to stay awake as they move freight through the dark American night. "A million miles," I whisper to myself, "all I've got to do is two-fifty." I nod off.

My firewood doused and buried, I am up and running long before sunup the next morning—striding beneath the charcoal black walls of Lava Canyon as though I'm still being chased; I am. Time and distance are vengeful hunters out here, and I am their skittish quarry. Still groggy from the damp, restless night, I flee mindlessly up one ridge line, come to an abrupt drop-off, turn tail, and backtrack. I pick up the creek bottom again and take it all the way to the Colorado River, never once looking back over my shoulder.

The wind is blowing, a light drizzle is sprinkling the glassine surface of the river, and the air temperature is in the upper fifties. Conditions notwithstanding, I must cross the *m 68* river to reach a food cache at the mouth of Tanner Canyon. From my rucksack I take my inflatable life vest, a cheap inner tube, and a beach ball. Even without putting my hand in it, I know the water is cold—in the low forties; I'll use the inner tube to keep me afloat, out of the water, while I paddle across the slick current below Lava Canyon Rapid (not *m 65.5* to be confused with Lava Falls 114 river miles downstream).

With increasing fear, I don the yellow U.S. diver's vest, blow up the small inner tube, then sit on it. But it doesn't have enough volume to keep me out of the water, so I pull it on like a swim-belt and start paddling across the river at Mile 65, towing my pack on the beach ball behind me.

It's not much more flotation than John Daggett and Bill Beers used when they "swam" 279 miles down the rapids-strewn Colorado River from Lee's Ferry to Pierce's Ferry in 1955. That was the year before the Colorado River Storage Project began constructing the porcine edifice of Glen Canyon Dam, an impediment some lifelong river runners once threatened to blow up and rename "Dominy Falls." Daggett and Beers slipped into the water on April 10, too early in the season—and too cold—for an ultramarathon river swim; they wore partial wet suits, wool underwear, swim fins, and Mae West life preservers. Barely two days into their epic swim, they wrecked on the midstream rock at President Harding Rapids, which left Daggett with "four or five deep cuts in his scalp and face—one a fraction of an inch from his eye—and a badly ripped knuckle on his right hand." But their main problem was not negotiating the river's powerful rapids; it was enduring the 53-degree water. In the August 5, 1955, issue of *Collier's Magazine,* Beers recounted: "Overexposure had chapped our hands so badly they bled, and our feet were painful from cuts and bruises. . . . Water leaking in through the rip in my shirt was making me unbearably cold." And throughout the twenty-six days the insurance salesmen spent negotiating the treacherous river in order to successfully complete their swim, they were repeatedly forced to get out and build fires in order to warm themselves.

But I am not trying to swim 279 miles of the Rio Colorado in the wake of Daggett and Beers; I am only trying to cross a few yards of it. Even with three seasons of river-running under my belt, however, I am still operating off the right side of my brain, as most distance runners do. And I am so groggy from sleep deprivation and physical fatigue, I am unable to foresee the consequences of my actions until I'm halfway across the icy river. Then, swimming madly, I realize that the inner tube around my waist is preventing me from ferrying across the current; instead, I am being swept helplessly downstream, my arms and legs now paralyzed with cold. The image comes to mind that my body will be found floating face down in an eddy somewhere between here and Phantom Ranch. I am too cold and enervated to continue. Fear seizes me: all the thought, training, and planning that went into this journey, and I am going to die.

Totally helpless, I turn and look at my pack. ANNERINO is stenciled on its back; eerily, it looks like my headstone bobbing down the current behind me. If they don't find my body, maybe they'll find my pack, the same way they found Boyd Moore's below Unkar Rapid. I take one last deep breath, lean back in my life vest, and paddle faintly before the bitter wave of death sweeps over me. But something catches my eye: my knife! For some reason—I'd never done it before—I have my knife strapped to the outside of my pack. I grab it, unsheathe it, and slash the vinyl anaconda wreathing around my waist. A gush of air bubbles breaks the surface of the gray river. The beast is dead.

I lift my arm out of the water to toss my knife into the river; I still am not going to make it, so why do I need the knife? For some unexplained reason, though, I stop mid-toss and abruptly resheathe the knife. It is then that I realize I am determined to survive. Never a master freestyler on any day, I breaststroke as hard as I can, hyperventilating as I try to sprint to the other side. With the inner tube deflated, I'm actually ferrying across the deadly current, and I don't stop breaststroking until I reach the wave of green tammies hanging over the sandy river bank. Without thinking, I clamber out of the soul-numbing water, put on my pack, and try running as hard as I can. If I stop to build a fire or to take off the life vest and slashed inner tube—if I attempt anything less than all-out physical effort—I will succumb to the final stages of hypothermia.

My steps are stumbles, though, slow groggy motion, as if I'm running in chain mail, but the direction is correct: west. And that's the direction in which I keep stumbling, fearing death if I falter and stop. One sloshy, leaden step slides wearily into the next, and the next, until, ever so slowly, I can feel my inner core rewarm from the forced effort.

m65.5.

I don't remember much about the four miles I stumble and lurch toward the mouth of Tanner Canyon, nor do I even notice the remains of George McCormick's 1904 Copper Grant Mine. I am stone cold, weary, and beaten. And by the time I finally reach the alluvial mouth of Tanner Canyon I am crying like a baby. I had been sucked into the icy specter of death and, for some reason unknown to me, the river gods had smiled upon me. But that's as far as I want to push this pathway. No more. I knew I could die trying to run the South Rim, before my inner Canyon pathway had tempered my naivete, and twice I had almost died of thirst on the shadow pathway of the Hopi-Havasupai Trail. But I am not willing now to pay the ultimate toll to run this desperate pathway. As far as I'm concerned, it's over. I'm out of this miserable, godforsaken canyon. End of story.

Still shivering like a jellyfish, I find my food cache in the middle of Tanner Wash fifteen minutes later; when I do, I see Chris May and Chris Keith staring at me with the same disbelief I feel upon seeing them. In the planning stages, the rendezvous were supposed to work this way, as they had on the inner Canyon and shadow pathways. But the reality of three people successfully linking up in this Canyon still startles me, especially this time out. I really hadn't been sure there was even going to be a food drop at Tanner, since the resupply crews were spread so thin. But *LIFE* magazine had generously provided Chris Keith with film and processing to cover this story, and on a wing and a prayer she and Chris May had volunteered to make the Tanner drop, in the hopes that she might get another picture for her photo essay, or be there in case something went wrong. So my news falls on sensitive ears, but she keeps shooting.

"It's over," I tell them both, tears and snot dripping off my chin. "I almost drowned crossing the river." They nod sympathetically, ask me the how and why of it, then stuff me into some dry clothes and a heavy down sleeping bag. I pass the rest of the gray, drizzly morning and afternoon recovering in their care, contemplating the decision I've made to abort this pathway. I'd admitted defeat on the North Rim once before, trying to walk this same route years earlier. It was a difficult decision then, but I'd lived with it. But that was backpacking, I tell myself, when you carried everything you needed; this is running, and there's no margin for error. Still, no matter what I do with my life from here on out, I'll never be in this position again. Part of me desperately wants to see this pathway to the end, but the other side of me doesn't want to die trying. I don't know; I'm torn.

Revitalized by hot soup, warm companionship, and my womblike sleeping bag, I wonder if the route beyond could possibly get any worse than what I've already been through trying to descend the Nankoweap and run the horrendous spine of the Butte Fault in one long day before facing the river. Major John Wesley Powell summed up the situation perfectly when he navigated the Colorado River through the Grand Canyon in 1869: "At one time, I almost concluded to leave . . . but for years I have been contemplating this trip. To leave the exploration unfinished, to say that there is a part of the Canyon which I cannot explore, having nearly accomplished it is more than I am willing to acknowledge and I determine to go on."

It was a good argument for Powell then, and it's a fair one for me now. But if I do decide to get out of this sleeping bag, I still have to recross the river, and I'm not prepared to risk my life trying to swim it again. Maybe I can find enough driftwood to build the sort of raft James White used. He was the sunburned and emaciated trapper and prospector who drifted up to the banks of Callville, Nevada, on September 7, 1867, claiming to have spent two weeks floating down the Colorado River in a desperate attempt to escape hostile Utes. If his incredible tale were true, that would make the thirty-year-old Colorado native the first man in history to have navigated the Colorado River through the Grand Canyon (albeit accidentally), two years before Major Powell's first successful expedition in 1869. Early admirers, like General William J. Palmer and Thomas F. Dawson, embraced White as a hero, believing that he had, indeed, come through the "Big Cañon", as I have come to believe. Others, like Major Powell and White's most disgruntled detractor, the promoter and railroad engineer Robert Brewster Stanton, said it was impossible for a man to negotiate more than five hundred miles of turbulent river currents and dangerous rapids on a hastily constructed raft in the time White claimed.

Two and a half weeks after being dragged out of the Colorado River at Callville, James White wrote a letter to his brother, describing his incredible ordeal:

> Navigation of the Big Canon
> *A Terrible Voyage*
> Callville, September.26.1867.
> Dear Brother it has ben some time senCe i have heard frome you i got no anCe from the last letter that i roat to you for i left soon after i rote i Went prospeCted with Captin Baker and gorge strole in the San Won montin Wee found vry god prospeCk but noth that Wold pay then Wee stare Down the San Won river wee travel down a bout 200 miles then Wee Cross over on Caloreado and Camp We lad over one day Wee found out that Wee Cold not travel down the river and our horse Wass Sore fite and Wee had may up our mines to turene baCk When Wei Was attaCked by 15 or 20 utes indis they Kill Baker and gorge Strole and my self tok fore ropes off from our hourse and a ax ten pounds of flour and our gunns Wee had 15 millse to woak to Calarado Wee got to the river Jest at night Wee bilt a raft that night Wee had good Sailing fro three days and the Fore day gorge strole Was

Wash off from the raft and down that left me alone i thought
that it Wold be my time next i then pool off my boos and
pands i then tide a rope to my wase I wend over falls from 10
to 15 feet hie my raft Wold tip over three and fore times a
day the thurd day Wee loss our flour flour and fore seven
days i had noth to eat to ralhhide nife Caber the 8. 9 days i
got some musKit beens the 13 days a party of indis frendey
they Wold not give me noth eat so i give my pistols for hine
pards of a dog i ead one of for super and the other breakfast
the 14 days i rive at Callville Whare i Was tak Care of by
James ferry i was ten days With out pants or boos or hat i
Was soon so burnt so i Cold hadly Wolk the ingis tok 7 head
horse from us Joosh i Can rite yu thalfe i under Went i see
the hardes time that eny man ever did in the World but
thank god that i got thrught saft i am Well a gin and i hope
the few lines Will fine you all Well i sned my beCk respeCk
to all Josh anCe this When you git it

DreCk yo letter to

Callville, Arizona

Josh ass Tom to anCy that letter i rote him sevel yeas a goe.

James White

To this day, no one knows for sure whether White or
Powell was "the first man through." But if White could
build a raft that would take him even partway down this
turbulent river, I figured I can build one to paddle a hundred
yards across it. Before I can advise my caring companions
of this idea, however, a group of river runners rows four
19-foot neoprene rafts into camp. By a stroke of incredible
fortune, I know one of the boatmen from having worked on
the river the previous summer. After patiently listening to
my own tale of woe, Wesley Smith offers me passage back
across the river. And suddenly the door to my dream swings
open again.

But I'm troubled. There is documented evidence that
the Paiutes "sometimes ventured into the Grand Canyon in
search of rock salt and mescal, and sometimes crossed . . .
[the river] to contact the Havasupai to the south." Even

when Powell went to investigate the murders of three of his 1869 expedition members, he learned that a group of Walapai "had chanced to cross the Colorado on a raft to visit their Shivwits [Paiute] friends." And neither the Walapai nor the Paiutes used sophisticated rafts. They swam the river or built a raft similar to White's. But those were pre-dam crossings, usually done in the summer when the water was low, relatively calm, and warm by comparison with today's icy river. Weighing those factors against the possibility of being fined by National Park Rangers for violating back-country regulation 36 CFR 2.1(a)1., which prohibits disturbance of natural features, such as collecting logs to build a raft, I accept Wesley's offer as being within the modern legal constraints of Grand Canyon National Park. And I turn in for the night.

Still chilled from the day before, I'm ready to run long before the sun bombs its way into the east end of the Canyon the next morning. After two days of damp, sleazy weather, I would embrace the fiery sun at this point, but a tumbling, gray wave of storm clouds is still frothing down off the North Rim. And I wonder whether I've embarked on this pathway a week or two too early. But the known water sources below the North Rim are even fewer and farther apart than those below the South Rim; thus Craig, Tim, and I purposely scheduled this run to coincide with what we've discovered is the Canyon's most fickle season: that narrow window between April and May, when inner Canyon weather systems can vacillate from blinding hail and snow to burning heat, and back again, within days; when the temperatures would, in theory, be moderate enough for biv-ouacing; and when the prospect of finding seasonal *tinajas* between perennial springs and creeks was greatest. I only hoped I wouldn't get too strung out between waterholes, the way I had the year before, when the sun finally laid in here for the summer.

Except for residual chills, I feel physically recovered from the near-drowning; emotionally, though, I'm reluctant to leave Chris May and Chris Keith. Once again my support crew has provided me with more emotional support than they know. They both assume everything will go as planned. "Don't worry," they tell me, "you've got it in the bag." I'm still plagued with doubts about reaching Phantom Ranch two to three sleeps west of here, but I try to muster a look of confidence for them as I wave good-bye and Wesley quietly rows me back across the calm and deadly river. I don't know whether I'll see them—or anyone else—again.

Between last year's river-running and this river crossing I've known Wesley only a few hours. The Colorado River boatman and Vietnam vet is tuned into the natural forces of the Canyon and the ways of Native Americans. And although he views my journey with some bewilderment, a bond has been forged, as if we're partners on a similar pathway. When we land on the opposite shore, we shake hands and wish each other luck.

I step out of the boat and strap on my pack and bota bags as Wesley ferrys back across the current. For a moment, self-doubt almost overwhelms me as I realize I've just burned my second bridge, but I try to shake it off as I skim along the Hakatai shale toward Unkar Creek. This near-ideal footing, however, soon turns into a jungle of tammies, arrow weed, coyote willow, and mesquite, and before long I am clawing my way through a vicious thicket, shaking out birds that flap noisily away at my approach.

Originally introduced into the United States from the Middle East in 1875, tammies were used for flood and erosion control along the lower Colorado River at the turn of the century. Like numerous other exotic species that have left their indelible marks on the Grand Canyon, the tammies migrated upriver year by year until they established a small foothold in the Canyon during the 1920s. That was decades before the completion of Glen Canyon Dam, back when wild spring runoff recharged beaches with sediment while simultaneously keeping the tammies in check. With the advent of the dam, however, the beaches began disappearing and the tammies proliferated with such intensity that the river corridor became choked with impenetrable jungles of this resilient plant.

It is just such a stand that I battle my way through during the first hour west of the Tanner, yelling, kicking, and swinging as if I were in a gang fight. When I finally emerge from this desperate thicket, my dark blue long johns are torn, my face is scratched, and any momentum I'd had has been stymied into an irritating lope. Nonetheless, I've reached Unkar Delta, one of the largest Anasazi habitation sites along the river corridor. Without stopping for a break, I start trudging up the steep, two thousand–foot ascent to a rock formation called The Tabernacle. It was a journey the Anasazi made each spring along this very route; having spent the winter on Unkar Delta growing corn, beans, and squash, they climbed back out to the North Rim to hunt deer, tan hides, and collect and roast agave hearts.

In *The Mountain Lying Down*, anthropologist Robert C. Euler speculated on what it might have been like for the Anasazi to make the same journey up from the river that I am now embarked on:

> The year was 1143 A.D. It was a raw spring day and a cold southwesterly wind was blowing as . . . two people slowly make their way up a precarious route from the canyon depths to the north rim. Each carried a large basket supported by a tumpline over the forehead, containing food— dried meat and the cooked and edible portion of the century plant—and skins filled with water. The man and woman were warmly dressed in loosely fitting cotton clothing covered with downy feathered robes. They wore heavy sandals made of yucca fibers.

It had taken them two days to walk out of the canyon. They had camped the previous night under a rock overhang that contained a small spring where they could replenish their water supply [before completing their journey to their summer dwellings atop the North Rim. These people were] thoroughly in tune with the rugged physical environment of the canyon and did not hold it in awe as many people do today.

. . . as I still do when I finally reach the eastern end of the Tonto formation near The Tabernacle barely the halfway point in the Anasazi's seasonal migrations. Unlike the fluted terrain of the Butte Fault, I am psychologically more comfortable with the broad terrace of the Tonto; having run its South Rim counterpart, I think I understand the nature of it. Still, this is the North Rim, *terra incognita* for most people, including myself, so I tread lightly across this uncompromisingly rugged and dangerous pathway, wondering what mysteries the North Rim will unveil for me today.

Two thousand feet below, I can still make out the faint outlines of Anasazi dwellings atop Unkar Delta, some of them eight- to ten-room masonry affairs. And I am still thinking about Euler's conclusions, "that human beings were able to adapt to the extreme terrain and to make a very good living in the canyon for about a hundred years . . . more people living in the Grand Canyon during the 12th century than there are today," when I realize that any understanding I'd gleaned from the South Tonto's extreme terrain two years earlier has little to do with the North Tonto. The reason soon becomes obvious; the South Rim, for the most part, drains away from the Canyon, whereas the North Rim drains, and thus erodes *into* it, thereby creating more free-standing rock temples like The Tabernacle and Zoroaster, and terraces and canyons far steeper and longer than those encountered below the South Rim. Thus the North Tonto not only is more rugged, it's also drier, narrower, and more precipitous. And because of the North Rim's heart-pounding exposure and physical relief, my running becomes a taxing mental effort. There is no disassociating from the physical act of running, a practice that had enabled me to dream my way most of the way across the South Tonto and the Hopi-Havasupai Trail. The terrain demands my utmost concentration, and the images I'm bombarded with and forced to respond to are both monotonous and life-threatening: step; don't knock the boulder down on you here; jump over a rock there; run around that cactus; don't fall to your death over there. There is no dream-filled reverie, no further musings about the Anasazi or any other historic or prehistoric mileposts. And the passage of time drags on and on. Yet if I lose my concentration, if I make one small mistake in this concerted running, I'll go down. And out here, that means forever. I continue heading west, running as hard as I can toward Vishnu Creek in hopes of reaching the next known water source before dark.

By sundown, I'm totally spent. I try simple math problems and fail to answer any of them. It is time to eat and sleep; but first, a fire. There is no debate tonight; I simply build one within the confines of Vishnu Amphitheater. I recline in its flickering warmth and stare up at the starry heavens backlighting the stark cathedral of 7,529-foot Vishnu Temple. Named by geologist Clarence Dutton for its mystical, come-hither quality, Vishnu forms the largest mountain within the Grand Canyon. Its needle-tipped summit reportedly was first climbed almost four decades before I struggled to the foot of it.

According to the Thursday, August 8, 1945, edition of *The Arizona Republican,*

> M. D. Clubb, of Stillwater, Okla., and his son, Rodger . . . after investigating the possibility of reaching the summit of Vishnu Temple two years ago . . . returned this year and succeeded in making the ascent [from the North Rim] on July 13,

1945. They found no evidence that it had been climbed before, and so were careful to leave a rock cairn with proper information. A few lizards and lichens comprised all the life found, but the views were magnificent.

Thirty-six years later, George Bain climbed Vishnu Temple solo from the Colorado River in one long, punishing day. But he also discovered something far more interesting then lizards and lichens during his October 23, 1981, ascent. The rare "metallic fossil" Bain found suggests that at least one of the Canyon's stupendous temples proved too tempting a target for U.S. Air Force pilots about the time Clubb and his son first climbed it. Nearing the summit after twelve continuous hours of climbing, George used his small pocket knife to remove a 50-caliber copper-jacketed tracer bullet from the white band of Coconino sandstone crowning Vishnu.

Dawn breaks, and I'm running, trailing far behind me images of George Bain, Anasazi hikers, James White, and my near-drowning. Time accelerates. Because I've crossed the threshold of the North Tonto, I now have one thing on my mind: to reach Clear Creek, the next perennial water source far to the west. Morning dissolves into afternoon, and I am still running when I finally reach it after descending a perilously steep chute from the Tonto. I stop, fill up my bags, and start running again. For the first time since leaving the Nankoweap Trail, I'm running along a modern path; it will lead me eight miles beyond to Phantom Ranch.

But if I'd longed to enjoy this stretch of trail, it's too late; I'm about to cave in to fatigue. I start stumbling, whimpering like a sniveling old fool, when I hear the motor drive of Chris Keith's camera. I'm not sure how much later it is. I'm caught off guard, but seeing her lifts my spirits—even though she doesn't have any food. She has crossed the threshold herself to photograph this desperate pathway, first by trekking in and out the Tanner, and now down the South

Kaibab and Clear Creek trails, more than forty miles thus far. After such a heroic effort, she understandably wants to take pictures. But my nerves are so frayed from running the North Tonto without falling that I fight the bit every step of the way, struggling once again at the foot of Zoroaster Temple. Again and again I break down from the struggle, but once I reach Bright Angel Creek at Phantom Ranch late that afternoon, I know it's over. I'm through, I tell myself; it's taken everything I had, mentally and physically, to reach this point, and I'm barely halfway.

Once again, Dick Yetman is there waiting for me. He has hiked all the way into the Canyon to run the next two days with me. Over a brew at the Phantom Ranch beer hall that evening, I tell him and another friend, Bob Farrell, that the risks are too great. I've already made too many mistakes, and I'm just an accident waiting to happen. They both nod and sip their beers as I stare silently at the other hikers who've struggled down into this seasonal war zone of limping and wounded canyoneers.

The next morning, I feel as if I've been run over by a truck. The last thing I want to do is get strung out on the North Tonto again. But Dick is determined. Perhaps a day of rest would do wonders, I tell him. Bob assures me it would. But Dick has to be back at work in three days. Work—what's that? It has no meaning down here, where the will to survive now dominates all my actions.

By 9 A.M. we are scrambling up the steep talus toward Utah Flats. Dick leads, taking the wrong turn once we've gained the Tonto two thousand feet above. After spending the next hour and a half backtracking, we head west on what we think is the right terrace. Having struggled alone for four days, it seems odd to run with someone else, and it is. But soon I realize Dick is sharing the burden of my weakness and our bond is sealed.

Having run what I estimate to be 80 to 85 percent of the first four days—the rest was devoted to stumbling or to climbing up and down—running is a movement that now seems totally out of character for the terrain we're crossing. I know it's just my exhaustion coloring my perception, since this is the same kind of terrain I ran the first four days. I struggle to maintain some semblance of a run, a trot, even a jog, but fatigue eventually forces me to bow down and walk. Periodically I make feeble attempts at running, for across the Canyon no more than a mile by way of the phantom crow I have a mirror. It is May, and I can see myself flying along the South Tonto forty-five miles from Hermit Creek to South Bass on one of the best running days of my life. Today I'm stumbling as hard and as fast as I can, led by a stranger and a friend.

Day 6: We are out of food and dangerously low on water, so we take advantage of the cool temperatures and start running before first light. Spring is turning to summer, however, and with the wonderful display of wildflowers comes the extremes of heat. We're not sure whether we'll find water before we run out, and it becomes a test of will to save at least a mouthful in each of our bota bags. Without water, we are completely at the mercy of this rim-locked desert.

It is dreary work, fighting my way through a mirage that may be induced by the heat refracting off the Tonto, by dehydration, or by both, but there's also a timeless beauty to it, as if I'm drifting in a dream cloud. And with each mile, whatever that means out here, my consciousness drifts from drudgery to dream and back again. *m9B*

By noon Crystal Creek is in sight. The two of us carefully drop off the steep Tonto and stumble down to the cool, trickling waters of the creek. We stay a long time, drinking like horses at a trough, not knowing where on the Tonto

m 99.3

above our next waterhole will be. We pay little attention to Crystal Rapid, the most feared rapid in North America.

That afternoon we struggle across what seems like the most difficult mile on the entire journey, the craggy section between Crystal and Tuna creeks; it is the only passage back up to the North Tonto and our way westward to the South Bass food drop that night. By late afternoon, however, we realize that South Bass is not in the cards. We make a dry camp west of Scorpion Ridge. There are canteens scattered about our camp; they are dry, melted to the Tonto like molten aluminum. They've been here since June 20, 1944, when "three men of the Army Air Corps parachuted into the Grand Canyon at night . . . when their B-24 bomber developed engine trouble."

We're starved for food, but they've cached no C-rations for us. We quickly root out a large lizard called a chuckwalla and kill it with a pointed stick, the same way the Anasazi did. Disheartening, yes, but the sight of the molten canteens drives home the desperation of our situation. Not that a lone chuckwalla will save our lives, but it's a symbol that the survival process must be initiated before it's too late. We roast the lizard over the coals, Anasazi-style, and Dick calls the spit-roasted flesh "chuck steak."

Day 7: We make another predawn start, running into the infinity of the west. Somewhere on the crimson horizon is the South Bass drop, but we don't reach it until late that morning, our throats parched, our bota bags empty, and our stomachs crying for food.

We are half a day late, and when we're spotted by our resupply team, bodies jump into action. Craig Hudson paddles across the river in a navy survival raft, towing a large air mattress behind him. He is not only our ferry back across the river but our caterer. He offers a bagful of bean burros, and we wolf through them before we utter word one.

Day 8: I feel completely abandoned. Dick Yetman, Craig Hudson, Tim Ganey, and Randy Mulkey have hiked out the South Bass. I am alone, again, struggling on the north side of the river, and that feels extremely odd after running—and surviving—with Dick for two days, especially after close friends provided an island of security for me in this inner-canyon frontier. It feels especially odd because I still can't see the "summit" of this inverted mountain pathway; if I hadn't seen it before, I would doubt the existence of that beautiful, roaring Thunder River pouring out of the Muav limestone.

M 108.5

My route takes me along the east bank of Shinumo Creek, past William Wallace Bass's old orchard to a dead end. The creek must be crossed, but it's too cold, too deep, and it's moving too fast. I inflate my life vest and run up and down the bank looking for a way across.

There's only one option and I take it, trying not to whimper when I think of how I'll be smashed before I drown when I fall in. So I don't hesitate. I hurl my pack twenty feet to the opposite shore. A cottonwood seedling is my bridge. I climb up it until it bends over an exposed rock at midcreek, hoping it doesn't snap. It doesn't, but it's not quite long enough. I'm forced to drop from its willowy upper branches onto the moss-covered rock. I touch down and slip, hugging the rock with both hands to keep from being swept into the deadly torrent. Gingerly I stand up and look at the jump I've got to make to get to the other side. There's no way; it's a good ten feet across. The farthest standing broad jump I ever did was a little over seven feet. There's only one thing to do; I can't reverse my move, even if I wanted to. I try not to think what it will feel like. I just dive, head first, arms outstretched, hoping I haven't misjudged the distance. Dust whirls, rocks fly.

I take the brunt of the fall on my rib cage, slamming the air out of me and banging my right hand. But I'm across.

≈ mill

I'm seized with loneliness and fear for the rest of the day as I struggle up the incipient North Bass "trail," but I make Muav Saddle by sundown.

m133

A temptation nearly overcomes me—and it's almost irresistible. No more than two miles away I know is a fire road. All I've got to do is walk up to it and follow it along the rim to the Thunder River trailhead. I could be there tonight. It would be over and nobody would blame me. But now I can finally see the summit or at least the final pitch leading to it. And I have to go on, although I desperately fear the uncertainty of what lies ahead.

Depressed at my commitment, I look around forested Muav Saddle for a level place to camp, and to my surprise discover an abandoned CCC cabin—with firewood *and* a bed. I throw my pack inside and sit on the front porch, watching the last of the sun's golden rays dance across the Canyon. This is it, I tell myself, the time of reckoning.

"Once in a lifetime, if one is lucky," Loren Eisley wrote in *The Immense Journey,* "one so merges with sunshine and air and running water that whole eons might pass in a single afternoon without notice."

Something akin to that extraordinary feeling envelops me when I wake the next morning. After eight days of struggling against myself and the forces of the Canyon, I suddenly feel as if this place has told me its secrets. I'm an insider, now, and the rest of my run will flow like the river, unimpeded by ego and self-doubt.

I bushwhack down densely wooded Saddle Canyon at a trot, dropping from one plunge pool of water to another as if I were put on this earth to do nothing but run. I feel strong, refurbished by the can of Hormel chili I found in the cabin the night before. Eating it out of that rusty can on that starlit porch was the best meal of my life. And this, I tell myself, will be the best running day of my life.

It is. The scrambling behind me, my movement is brisk and sure-footed. I take in deep rhythmic gulps of cool fresh air. What a day to be alive and running! I'm gushing with joy and excitement. I can see the summit and the end of a five-year dream; the trilogy will be complete once I cross Tapeats Creek. **M 1 3 3**

I follow the right bank, higher and higher, hoping to skirt Tapeats Narrows, but my path deadends. I backtrack. There's only one option.

I blow up my vest again, and with my pack strapped to my back leap across the swollen channel. But I'm too care-free and I miss, sliding ten feet down the bare rock and splashing into the torrent. Clear-headed, I struggle. There will be no drowning today, I tell myself. Using my feet in front of me to take the brunt of each boulder, I grab the limb of a tree fifty yards downstream and drag myself out. I stand up and, seeing that I'm unharmed, jump up and down, waving my hands over my head in triumph.

It's all falling together, I tell myself. I can taste sweet victory a half hour away. When I reach the confluence of Tapeats Creek and Thunder River, however, I see there is no way to ford the two creeks below the confluence. Fear takes over again, but I try to rein it. I see clearly what will happen if I make a mistake. To compound matters, *if* I successfully cross Tapeats Creek I still have to cross Thunder River, and that looks worse.

I'm stuck.

I try wading across Tapeats Creek above the conflu-ence, but once it gets chest-deep I back out.

Okay, I tell myself, burn your last bridge. I throw my pack across the creek swollen with snowmelt and look for a proper vaulting pole; not that I've ever pole-vaulted before, but I can't let that stop me now.

The best thing I come up with is the semigreen stalk of

a century plant about ten feet long. I pull some splinters off, then trot back to what looks like a suitable launch pad. I stick the stalk in the torrent, but the end of it is swept downstream before it touches bottom. If I can put enough body pressure on it to gain purchase, maybe I can arch forward.

There are no other options I'd like to consider. Gripping the top of the pole tightly with both hands, I plant the pole and dive for the other side. As soon as the pole jars against the bottom, I hear a crack, then a snap. The pole breaks, hurling me against the opposite bank shoulder first. I grab desperately, repeatedly missing the exposed roots of a cottonwood as I'm swept helplessly downstream toward the maelstrom of the confluence. A thud jars my right hip. I cough up air, then grab the large root that finally stops me.

How many more times will this happen? I look up at the quarter-mile-long Thunder River cascading like a rampaging flash flood down into Tapeats Creek at a forty-five-degree angle. No way to cross that.

I pick up my pack and start scrambling up the steep right bank, wondering if I can't somehow traverse above the falls. Suddenly, I see that the door has swung open again. A large, moss-covered cottonwood bridges this short and awesome river. After five years, the dream has finally become a reality. I step across. It is over.

When I see Tim, Randy, and Chris at the foot of Thunder River, there is only one thing to say, and I scream it: "WE'RE OUTTA' HERE!"

EPILOGUE

The Real World

Haniel Long once wrote: "If a person does not fear to look into the Canyon and see distance such as he has never seen elsewhere, depth such as he has never dreamt of, and if he becomes lost in shades of gentian and cherry and trout-like silver, watches the unceasing change of hue and form in depth, distance, and color, he will have feelings that do not well go into words and are perhaps more real on that account."

For years after Tim, Craig, and I walked away from the North Rim, I would not—could not—go back to the Grand Canyon. I feared looking into it. I'd never tried to cross such a distance before, through so frightening a depth. And the fact that I'd followed, and survived, pathways that bridged the threshold between both marked me in ways I couldn't explain in words. The paths were dreamways, really, nothing more, because the Canyon remains unmarked by my crossings. What does remain is the lifelong kinship I feel toward the kind, selfless friends and others who helped me, in one way or another, fulfill an impossible dream. To them this book is also dedicated.

I would like to thank my family, Dave Ganci, Dick Yetman, Chris Keith, Tony Ebarb, Chris May, George Bain, Silvio Sirias, Jim Hills, Bob Farrell, Jack Cartier, Gary Drysmala, Mike Johnson, Rich Nebeker, Kimmy Johnson, Ginny Taylor, Bob Mansky, Brian Gardner, Margie Erhart, Alan Weisman, Rex Woods, Randy Mulkey, Bill Heywood, Ann Johnson, John Schroeder, Sonia Sunshine, Wesley Smith, Norm Tessman, Dennis Casebier, Doug Kasian, Harvey Butchart, Jim Gaston, Geary Redmond, Louise Teal, Chuck Bowden, Bill Broyles, and Mel Scott; the Arizona Historical Society (Tucson), and the University of Arizona Special Collections; the Indian Nations of the Tohono O'odham, Pima, Maricopa, Apache, Yavapai, Hopi, Navajo, Havasupai, Mojave, and Chemehuevi; the good people at Harbinger House for taking a chance on me; Tony Mangine for his "Hail Mary" catch, and for first showing me the way to long distance running; Dick Vonier for keeping the wolf from the door while this was going to press; Mike Thomas for leading me through the storm, and for his unwavering friendship; 'Mando for his sense of humor; and to Elle, for reasons that never need explaining.

Selected Bibliography

ANNERINO, JOHN. *Adventuring in Arizona*. San Francisco: Sierra Club Books, 1991.

———. *High Risk Photography: The Adventure Behind the Image.* Helena: American & World Geographic Publishing, 1991.

———. *Hiking the Grand Canyon.* San Francisco: Sierra Club Books, 1986.

———. "Path of Fire," Phoenix: *Phoenix Magazine,* Sept. 1991.

BASSO, KEITH, ed. *Western Apache Raiding and Warfare.* Tucson, Ariz.: University of Arizona Press, 1971.

BLOFELD, JOHN. *Mantras: Sacred Words of Power.* New York: E.P. Dutton, 1977.

———. *The Secret and Sublime.* London: Allen & Unwin, 1973.

BOARDMAN, PETER. *The Shining Mountain.* New York: Vintage Books, 1985.

CASEBIER, DENNIS. *The Mojave Road.* Norco, Calif.: Tales of the Mojave Road Publishing, 1975.

CHATWIN, BRUCE. *The Songlines.* New York: Viking, 1987.

DAVID-KNEEL, ALEXANDRA. *The Magic and Mystery in Tibet.* Secaucus, N.J.: University Books, 1965.

DRAEGER, DON F., and ROBERT W. SMITH. *Asian Fighting Arts.* New York: Berkley Medallion Books, 1974. Originally published in 1969 by Kodansha International Ltd.

FLETCHER, COLIN. *The Man Who Walked Through Time.* New York: Alfred K. Knopf, 1968.

GOVINDA, LAMA ANAGARIKA. *The Way of the White Clouds.* Boulder, Colo.: Shambala Publications, 1966.

GREG, HERMAN. *Tales from the Mohaves.* Norman, Okla.: University of Oklahoma Press, 1970.

HUGHES, J. DONALD. *The Story of Man at the Grand Canyon.* Grand Canyon, Ariz.: Grand Canyon Natural History Association, 1967.

JAMES, GEORGE WHARTON. *The Grand Canyon of Arizona: How to See it.* Boston: Little, Brown, & Co., 1905.

————. *In and around the Grand Canyon; The Grand Canyon of the Colorado River in Arizona.* Boston: Little, Brown, and Co., 1900.

LAIRD, CAROBETH. *The Chemehuevi.* Banning, Calif.: Malki Museum Press, 1976.

LEONARD, GEORGE. *The Ultimate Athlete.* New York: Avon Books, 1974.

MESSNER, REINHOLD. *The Big Walls.* London: Kaye & Ward Ltd., 1978.

MURPHY, MICHAEL, and RHEA A. WHITE. *The Psychic Side of Sports.* Reading, Mass.: Addison-Wesley, 1978.

MUSASHI, MIYAMOTO. *A Book of Five Rings, (Go Rin No Sho).* Trans. Victor Harris. New York: The Overlook Press, 1974. Written in 1645.

On the Trail of the Spanish Pioneer: The Diary and Itinerary of Francisco Garcés, 1775–1776. Trans. Elliott Coues. New York: E.P. Harper, 1900.

ORTIZ, ALFONSO, ed. *Handbook of North American Indians: Southwest.* Vol. 10. Washington, D.C.: Smithsonian Institution, 1983.

PATTIE, JAMES OHIO. *Personal Narrative of James Ohio Pattie.* Cleveland, Ohio: Arthur H. Clark Company, 1905.

PEATTIE, RODERICK, ed. *The Inverted Mountains: Canyons of the West.* New York: Vanguard Press, 1948.

RAWICS, SLAVOMIR. *The Long Walk.* New York: Lyons & Burford, 1984.

SIMMONS, LEO W. *Sunchief: The Autobiography of a Hopi Indian.* New Haven, Conn., and London: Yale University Press, 1942.

SUZUKI, DAISETZ TEITARO. *The Training Of The Zen Buddhist Monk.* Berkeley: Wingbow Press, 1974. Originally published in Kyoto in 1934.

TASKER, JOE. *Savage Arena.* New York: St. Martin's Press, 1982.

TOHEI, KOICHI. *Aikido in Daily Life.* Tokyo: Rikugei Publishing House, 1966.

UNDERHILL, RUTH, DONALD M. BAHR, BAPTISTO LOPEZ, JOSE PANCHO, and DAVID LOPEZ. *Rainhouse and Ocean: Speeches for the Papago Year.* Flagstaff, Ariz.: Arizona Museum of Northern Arizona Press, 1979.

ABOUT THE AUTHOR

John Annerino is a photojournalist whose work has been published in *Life, Time, Newsweek,* and *New York Times Magazine,* among many others; he is represented by the Gamma-Liaison picture agency in New York and Paris and the Marka agency in Milano. Annerino is the author and photographer of five books, including *High Risk Photography: the Adventure Behind the Image* (American & World Geographic Publishing). He is currently photographing *Canyons of the Southwest* for Sierra Club Books.